WILD
FLOWER
GARDENING

D1397850

WI
LIFE & LEISURE

WILD FLOWER GARDENING

John Chambers

WI BOOKS LTD

Acknowledgements
The author would like to thank
Geoff Ellis for his assistance.

Editors Suzanne Luchford and Anna Mumford
Commissioning Editor Hilary Wharton
Line illustrations Wendy Bramall
Picture research Julia Golding
Photographs opposite the following pages: Dr Kevan Chambers pp 32, 48
inset above and below, 64 above left and below, 65 main photograph and
inset, 112; Gales Honey page 33; Wildlife Matters Photographic Library
pp 16, 17 main photograph and inset, 48 main photograph, 96, 97 main
photograph and insets above and below, 113, 128, 129, 144 above and
below, 145; World Wildlife Fund, David Black page 49 above; World
Wildlife Fund, Brian Massey page 49 below left and right; World Wildlife
Fund, Nicky White, page 64 inset above.
Cover photography by Jhon Kevern
Designed by Anita Ruddell
This edition produced by Ward Lock (Publishers) Ltd
8 Clifford Street, London W1X 1RB, an Egmont Company

Published by WI Books Ltd
39 Eccleston Street
London SW1W 9NT

British Library Cataloguing in Publication Data
Chambers, John L. (John Laurence)
Wild flower gardening
1. Gardens. Ornamental wild flowering
plants. Cultivation
I. Title
635.9'676

ISBN 0-947990-45-3

First published 1989
© WI Books Ltd 1989

All rights reserved. No part of this publication may be
reproduced, stored in a retrieval system, or transmitted in
any form or by any means, electronic, mechanical,
photocopying, recording or otherwise without the prior
permission of the copyright owner.

Text set in Goudy Old Style by MS Filmsetting Limited, Frome, Somerset
Colour reproduction by Tennon and Polert Colour Scanning Ltd, Hong Kong
Printed and bound in Great Britain by
Hazell, Watson & Viney Ltd,
Member of the BPCC Group, Aylesbury, Bucks

WI Life & Leisure Series
The Complete Book of Home Preserving by Mary Norwak
Home-made Wines, Cordials & Syrups by Dr F. W. Beech
A Guide to Countryside Conservation by Dr John Feltwell

LIST OF CONTENTS

Welsh poppy

INTRODUCTION

*I*n recent years, there has been a tremendous increase in wild flower gardening. The first enthusiasts were wild flower lovers, conservationists and keen horticulturists, but before long the general public were increasingly eager to introduce wild flowers into their gardens, for a variety of worthwhile reasons. Some gardeners grow nostalgic favourites such as cowslip or primrose, or attractive and well-liked species which were once locally or nationally common. Others want to create mini-countryside habitats or make their gardens more attractive to wildlife, especially butterflies and birds. For many years, conservation organisations, the media and leading personalities have not only promoted the use of wild flowers in gardens but also increased awareness of the dangers they face in the wild.

Wild flowers may be integrated with cultivated flowers or grown in areas entirely devoted to native plants and work well in any size garden. In fact grown under garden conditions, wild flowers often reveal horticultural merits not always apparent in their native surroundings. When grown free of competition from invasive grass and other plants, they are often able to establish themselves much faster, and produce more flowers with larger petals which bloom over a longer period. There have always been some wild flowers grown in gardens and they are currently being joined by many more varieties of equal merit in a surge of interest which this book aims to strengthen.

SAVING
WILD FLOWERS

When did you last walk in natural, unspoilt countryside and see a massive display of native wild flowers? Apart from the furthest reaches of the highlands and islands, increasingly we are now surrounded by intensively used agricultural land, amenity grassland and either state or privately-run regimented woodlands and forest.

Luckily, not all the wild flowers have disappeared. We can still enjoy the heather on the wilder hills and coasts. Traditional bluebells still brighten many woodlands in spring. Enough harebells remain to give a summer blue sheen to the remnants of the traditional chalk downlands. Cow parsley is a glorious delight alongside many country lanes and roadsides, though sometimes rather hazardous for motorists. Take a train ride and you will find the white trumpets of the larger bellbine flowering much as they always did on boundary hedges and fences.

The various conservation bodies must be given great credit for what they have done to maintain and re-establish the natural life of the countryside. By maintaining areas such as a spring-flowering fritillary meadow in Suffolk they have also helped save some of the rarer wild flowers from extinction – even though the pressure of visitors often leads to some much needed control of access.

However, many of the common wild flowers known to our parents and grandparents get harder and harder to find. The once common buttercup-yellow corn marigold, pink corncockle and blue cornflower have been virtually eradicated from crops of cereals by increasingly efficient herbicides. Even an occasional field display of the annual red or common poppy, that most tenacious survivor, usually only follows a bout of inefficient farm spraying, whilst wet-loving meadowsweet and cuckooflower (lady's smock) have been lost from many areas following field drainage.

It has been calculated that of the 1,500 or so natural wild flower species in the British Isles, the future of 300 or so is seriously threatened and probably at least ten have already been lost in fairly recent times. In terms of the national economy this probably matters very little, however, if we care about the wonderfully rich natural flora we have inherited we should start thinking of ways to stop the losses increasing.

It is all too easy to complain about changes in the countryside without attempting to understand why they have occurred. During the past 50 years we have lived through an agricultural revolution, probably more far-reaching than anything that has happened in our history. Coupled with the enormous loss of land to housing and industry, changes in farming practices have altered the face of these islands more than at any time since the Enclosure Acts of the eighteenth century. The effects are only too obvious.

For the past half-century farmers and foresters have been encouraged and paid to be more efficient. This has helped increase the amount of home-grown food and timber and reduce the bill for imports. In this, they have undoubtedly been successful, though at some considerable cost to the environment. With increased efficiency has come over-production and there is every possibility that at least some of the poorer land will eventually be taken out of crop production. It cannot be assumed, however, that land 'set aside' from agriculture will be allowed to return to its 'natural' state. As a valuable national resource it is bound to be used for something; one possibility is the production of quick-growing and heavy-yielding plants ('biomass') to give an alternative to fossil fuels.

At the same time, the countryside is also being used increasingly for leisure, especially the more beautiful parts. Here again there are dangers from over-use which are already apparent in some areas. Too many people using a limited facility for their enjoyment brings a strong probability of wildlife and its associated ecology being irreparably damaged.

With the increased loss of the traditional countryside has come much greater public concern. Many farmers have now become more conservation minded as they come to realise the benefits to them of a better balanced countryside. In fact, though there are still black areas, there is now much more general agreement that our countryside is in danger and greater co-operation between those concerned to help restore the balance.

For example, although some field hedges are still being removed, others, where they fit into modern farming patterns and management, are being replaced or restored. Many native broad-leaved trees have been planted recently in field corners and along headlands. Encouraged by environmentalists, a number of farmers and landowners are now either actually sowing wild flower mixtures or leaving headlands uncultivated to help encourage natural regeneration.

All this takes time; we cannot expect to restore the countryside overnight and in many areas probably we never will. So what can we, who are probably not large landowners but who care about preserving our native wildlife, do about it? Personally, we can have little effect on the total environment but we can help at least to preserve many of the best wild flower species by growing them in our gardens. An important side effect is that we will then help maintain other forms of wildlife such as birds, bees, butterflies and many beneficial insects.

The total area of the private gardens in this country comes to a staggering figure of over one million acres. This is about one-fiftieth of all the land in the country – more than six times all the national nature reserves and not much less than all the special sites of scientific interest (SSSIs) put together. If only a small proportion of these gardens grew a collection of wild flowers this would ensure that many of them are saved for the future. The purpose of this book is to help explain how to do this.

• WILD FLOWERS AS GARDEN PLANTS •

First of all it is important to realise that our native wild flowers are not exotic, nor are they very different from many of our normal garden plants. Before breeders took over and either crossed them with other species or selected out what they thought were desirable colours and shapes, they were all the flowers we had.

As collectors roamed the world, however, it became fashionable to grow many more of the plants they brought home, even though some of them were expected to grow at or beyond the limit of their normal climatic range. In the wave of increased gardening interest throughout the nineteenth and twentieth centuries many of our native flowers, though by no means all, were forgotten.

Many country-dwellers remained faithful to our home-grown plants. When they were more plentiful, many wild flowers like the cowslip, oxeye daisy, bluebell, columbine, foxglove and primrose were often either dug up and transplanted or spread naturally to cottage gardens. Being native, they usually naturalised easily and there was little danger of loss through adverse climatic conditions. There many can still be seen, growing happily just like any other garden plant.

Taking wild flowers out of their natural environment and putting them into gardens reveals an interesting fact. Although not usually changing in character, by removing the intense natural competition you will find they often make much better plants. This in turn leads to more flowers with larger petals flowering over a longer season.

Competition is, of course, quite normal in the wild and nature's law of the survival of the fittest can be one reason why some species predominate in certain areas, others being local soil type and situation. In more recent years management of the countryside, or lack of it, plus changing circumstances have increased this competition. The lack of regular hedge trimming, stubble burning, less 'free range' grazing, loss of rabbits and other plant-eating wild animals and the spread of more aggressive cultivated grasses and other coarse agricultural plants have all helped to stifle a flora which developed originally under very different conditions. As a result of this, many of the flowers which remain are not always seen at their best.

In fact, it can come as a surprise to know that wild flowers often need quite careful management. Left untended the countryside may at first provide a flush of bloom but, certainly on the better soils, in our climate it will soon degenerate into a coarse scrub of trees and bushes over a thick undergrowth of largely unattractive plants. This can often be seen in dense, badly managed woodland where relatively few wild flowers usually survive.

So if you plant wild flowers in your garden you might be surprised at how well they grow and the display they provide. A wide range of them, of which ragged-robin, oxeye daisy, foxglove, cowslip and the related oxlip, musk mallow and meadow crane's-bill are but a small selection, can in fact rival many of the horticultural merits of often closely related native and imported garden flowers. Being naturally hardy under our conditions, they will often last longer.

A word of caution, however, although fitting in well with most common garden plants, being natural survivors some wild flowers can be invasive and will need some control if they are to mix happily with their neighbours. Some, like many garden plants, will need lifting and splitting regularly to keep them to shape and size; a number, feverfew and oxeye daisy are good examples, must be dead-headed (removal of the flowerheads) regularly to stop them seeding all over the garden.

Although often quite tolerant of soil and conditions, as with most plants, wild flowers have their likes and dislikes. Many will grow well in open borders, others growing wild in woodlands or marshes need more care in choice of situation. Some need specifically acid or alkaline soil conditions (see pages 69–132).

Like many other plants, wild flowers usually grow best in the garden in clumps of three or four together, rather than as single specimens. Similarly, it is usually best to divide perennials and biennials from annuals like corn marigold, corncockle, cornflower and field poppy, which are worth a separate bed or part of the border.

However, you alone can decide how you want to grow wild flowers in your garden. Try picking some favourites and see how they succeed. Just as you would, in fact, with any other garden plant.

♦ WILD GARDENS ♦

Once you have found what a good garden display wild flowers provide, or perhaps have become hooked on them (it happens), you might like to go further and establish a separate wild flower garden. This is especially suitable for plants needing rather special situations like woodlands or marshes and which might not grow so well in the open border.

Many gardens have a corner shaded by trees, walls or fences and this makes a good habitat for natural woodland plants. Good species to grow there include foxgloves, bluebells, the blue periwinkle (good

Wild pansy

ground cover), shiny-leaved woodruff with white flowers, sweet violet and the golden lesser celandine. To grow over a fence with roots in the shade but flowers in the sun, plant the native wild honeysuckle and, if you have plenty of room, the wild clematis known as traveller's-joy or old man's-beard.

A wet spot in the garden or the margins of a pond can be used for a collection of marsh plants such as the beautiful lilac-flowered cuckoo-flower or lady's-smock, creamy-white meadowsweet, the golden marsh-marigold or kingcup and the slender spikes of purple-loosestrife. Although some of these will also succeed as border plants, especially on very heavy soils, they need plenty of moisture round the roots to grow really well. Ways of creating a simple mini-marsh for moisture-loving plants, either as part of a border or by extending the margins of a pond are suggested on pages 40–4.

The base of a large tree can also be used to create an attractive small wild garden. Flowers like the primrose, sweet violet, dog-violet, the delicate pinky-white wood anemone and wood-sorrel grow well together, or can be mixed with spring-flowering bulbs like snowdrops, species crocus, anemone blanda and dwarf narcissus. For later in the summer follow with herb-robert, nettle-leaved bellflower and red campion, which all tolerate semi-shade and dry conditions.

Gardens solely or predominantly planted with wild flowers can, in fact, be created in many soils and situations. Remember, however, that they will need managing like a normal garden. In particular, the balance of flowering and colour will only be maintained if the strongest species are prevented from taking over from the weakest.

Do not forget that even wild flowers have weeds! Invasive perennial species like couch grass, creeping thistle and creeping buttercup can be as obnoxious as when among any other plants. As with normal garden plants, they are best controlled before the soil is planted. Annual weeds should be less of a problem, especially if a mix of plants is chosen to give good ground cover to provide competition.

A number of wild flowers are, however, prolific seeders and unless dead-headed some like herb-robert, feverfew, ragged-robin and oxeye daisy can quickly colonise throughout the garden. This can turn them into 'a plant growing in the wrong place', the classic definition of a weed

– though it can equally be said of a number of garden plants which are allowed to go to seed.

There is, therefore, no need to be put off growing wild flowers, whether in your borders or as a separate wild garden, because you think they might take over. A few might but this book does not recommend them and they are, in any case, not usually the most attractive to grow in gardens. Provided, in fact, that you grow and care for wild flowers as you would any other plants, they will mostly act like any garden plant and give many hours of pleasure.

◆ MINI-MEADOWS ◆

Most gardens contain a lawn or at least a patch of grass and this can be a good place to grow some of the sun-loving meadow wild flowers. In fact, if a lawn is left unsprayed it will often be colonised quite quickly by several rosette or low-growing species such as bird's-foot-trefoil, dandelion, plantains, speedwell, daisy and clovers. These will be regarded as weeds by many gardeners but unless you require a bowling green, croquet lawn or other fine surface there really is little need to eradicate them. If you do not want them all over the lawn, they could perhaps be left undisturbed in one corner or around the edges.

Although some of these plants spread vegetatively, you can encourage the bulbous buttercup, plantains, dandelion and daisy to seed themselves by raising the height at which the grass is cut during and just after the flowering season. Other wild flowers like the hawkbits, hawkweeds, lady's bedstraw, cinquefoils and yarrow can be raised from seed or bought as plants and planted into the sward. To allow them time to establish, this is best done in the autumn after regular mowing has finished or well before it starts in spring.

Undoubtedly the best way to appreciate natural grassland flowers is to sow them down in a mixture with suitable grasses and create your own flowering mini-meadow. One advantage of a mini-meadow is that it will require considerably less cutting. Suggested mixtures for a range of soils and sites are given on pages 142–4. Like border wild flowers, species can be chosen to give a range of flowers throughout the spring and summer, for various soils and situations or to encourage butterflies, bees and other insects plus birds and small mammals.

A mini-meadow does not need to cover a large area. It could take over from any areas of less well-tended grass already in a garden, under fruit trees, as paths leading from one part of the garden to another or next to hedges. Remember, however, that such a mixed sward must be managed correctly to prevent the grasses taking over and the area reverting to a rough sward.

Part of this management is to grow the wild flowers with fine-leaved and thinly-sown grasses which are not over-vigorous or do not need too much cutting. Unless your garden is on a naturally poor soil like a sandy heath, most natural rough swards often consist of very coarse and vigorous species like couch, Yorkshire-fog, rye-grass and other agricultural grasses. Although the flowers can be planted directly into the sward, it is usually best to create a mini-meadow on bare soil by sowing a suitable mixture of wild flowers and grasses.

Several different lawn grasses can be used, but some species and varieties sold for sports turf or agricultural grasses grazed by animals are too aggressive. They smother the wild flowers and need too frequent cutting – either of which can lead to the important wild flower/grass balance being lost. The most suitable species for mini-meadows include browntop, chewing's fescue, sheep's fescue and red fescue but even these must be sown at a much lower rate than for an ornamental lawn.

The other important part of sward management is to cut it to the right height at the right time. The aim should be to simulate the conditions of a cycle of grazing by animals, and cutting for hay under which most of the meadow flowers developed. This will both keep the grass under reasonable control and allow the flowers to self-seed and so regenerate.

◆ HERBS AND WILD FLOWERS ◆

After asking what is the difference between wild flowers and weeds, the next question most often asked by newcomers to wild flower gardening is: 'Well, what really is the difference between herbs and wild flowers?' The answer is often 'not a lot', especially for a number of our native plants and wild flowers. Look in many seed catalogues; or visit a mixed herb and wild flower garden and you will find a number of herbs such as tansy, wormwood, marjoram, chives, salad burnet, green fennel, sweet woodruff and many others gathered for centuries from the countryside for their culinary or medicinal uses. Some of them are still quite widely used, though nowadays more in the kitchen than as medicine, several are also worth a place in the border as good garden plants. A most interesting bed can be made consisting solely of useful native plants. Unless they are to be kept as a collection or for visual effect it might, however, be best to keep kitchen herbs separate from the others – or you might get some peculiar results!

As a rule it is generally best not to let herbs you wish to use produce flowers and set seed but to maintain their vegetative growth for as long as possible. Chives in full flower, for example, make a very attractive edging to many cottage garden paths but the de-blossoming of a few plants is essential to keep a supply of young leaves for flavouring a salad.

Native herbs, like most other wild flowers, generally set seed in abundance so will need dead-heading to stop them spreading around the garden. This can, however, sometimes be an advantage as you find them springing up in cracks, crevices, and walls in most unusual places.

CULTIVATION OF
WILD FLOWERS

· PREPARATIONS FOR CULTIVATING ·
WILD FLOWERS

Wherever you intend growing your wild flowers, to be successful the preparations before sowing or planting should be just as thorough as with any other garden plants.

If you intend to add wild flowers to a mixed border, for example, you must make sure there is sufficient room and that the young plants will not be over-grown early in life by vigorous neighbours. If the soil structure is poor it should be improved by forking in peat, fine bark or compost plus a light dressing of a general fertilizer. This will help retain water in dry weather and prevent competition for moisture and nutrients from plants already growing in the border.

In addition, make sure that you have placed the plants with due regard to height and spread so that the wild flowers will not over-grow the other plants in the border or be dominated by them. Note that the heights given in reference books are usually the average which a plant will achieve in the wild. As mentioned earlier, this can be exceeded by several inches in fertile garden soils and with less natural competition. You will also save yourself considerable work later by not placing vigorous ground coverers such as wild strawberry or bird's-foot-trefoil next to rosette-forming plants, such as cowslip and primrose, which they can quickly smother.

If you are creating a new bed especially for wild flowers, perhaps out of a lawn, the preparations need to be thorough and you will need to take plenty of time. In particular, eradicate as thoroughly as possible perennial weeds like couch, docks, bindweed, nettles and thistles. They will produce a natural flora of sorts but almost certainly not the one you want. Although they can be kept under control after planting by the careful use of chemical weedkillers, removal before planting is far less time consuming.

Given time and foresight, a really weedy patch can be sprayed or watered with the systemic herbicide Tumbleweed (glyphosate), which deals effectively with deep roots of weeds like bindweed and creeping thistle – difficult to remove completely by mechanical means. It is also particularly effective against all grasses, so keep the spray well clear of any adjacent grass or lawn.

Give the weedkiller about a month to work and then fork over the ground thoroughly, incorporating at the same time a generous dressing of compost. After digging, tread the soil down to get a firm plant or seedbed and rake in a general fertilizer such as the inorganic Growmore or organic blood, fish and bonemeal. The next step is to make a plan of the bed and mark out where all the different plants are to go, leaving plenty of room between different species. A good rule of thumb is to allow half as much room between each type of plant as their expected height. Plants of the same species should be planted in clumps rather closer together.

The preparations for a flowering mini-meadow will need to be even more thorough than if just sowing grass. Ideally the soil should not be too rich and areas where the fertility has been built up for several years for vegetable gardening are best avoided. Old herbaceous borders that have been let go often provide a good site, once all the old plants and weeds are removed.

If the area being sown is already grassed, the turf is best removed before digging or rotovating to prepare the seed bed. This will help lower the fertility of the soil and remove any risk of re-growth from unwanted grasses. Where fertility is naturally low, grass and broad-leaved perennial weeds can be eradicated with Tumbleweed.

As with sowing any type of grass, the importance of establishing a firm seedbed for a mini-meadow cannot be over-emphasised. This will only be achieved by preparing the soil in plenty of time, so that it settles naturally before giving a final raking to level it just before seeding. This also encourages annual weeds to germinate early and reduces later competition. Any weeds which grow ahead of the grass/wild flower can be removed by careful hand weeding but most will disappear with later mowing.

Many of the wild flower seeds in a mini-meadow mixture, for example harebell, are very small and will only germinate successfully if sown on a surface rather finer than normally used for grass seed. If there is a danger of this leading to surface capping (an impenetrable soil surface), which can occur especially on soils high in silt, rake in fine sedge peat during the final preparation of the seedbed. *Never* use fertilizers of any kind on a mini-meadow.

• TREATMENT OF WILD FLOWER SEEDS •

Given the right conditions most wild flower seeds germinate easily, though they can sometimes be erratic. However, if you look at the growing instructions on the packets of some species, you will find that some need a cold spell before they will germinate satisfactorily. This applies in particular to all primulas (primrose, cowslip and oxlip) and a number of other popular flowers including bluebell, both sweet and dog violets and ramsons (wild garlic). Technically, this process is known as stratification or vernalisation and even where a cold spell is not essential, there are several species such as the harebell and its relative the nettle-leaved bellflower and columbine where it will often give better results.

The natural way to stratify seed is to imitate nature by sowing it in the autumn and allowing the weather to provide a natural cold spell. An alternative method, especially for the more expensive seeds, is to sow in pots or boxes which are then stood in a cold frame for the winter, preferably sunk in the soil. After germination the seedlings are dealt with normally.

Sometimes, especially if the winter has been very mild, it can take a second cold spell to make the seeds germinate. There are some species which need one cold period, followed by warmth, followed by another cold spell; this is known as double-dormancy. So never throw away seed pans or hoe up drills without giving them another chance. In fact, many wild flower seeds germinate in batches and a second flush of seedlings can often follow some time after the first. You will, however, need to identify the latecomers by keeping them well labelled.

An alternative to giving a natural cold spell is to provide an artificial period of stratification. Mix the seed with several times its bulk in a good grade of moist silver sand and place it in a sealed polythene bag in the coldest part of a refrigerator, but not the ice-box. A small bag of washed silver sand can be bought quite cheaply in any good garden shop or centre. Take the seed out of the refrigerator after a period of 6 to 12 weeks and sow it together with the sand either in an outdoor drill, covering in the normal manner, or in a pot or box in a cold greenhouse. As some species, harebell is one, might start to germinate whilst in the refrigerator, handle them carefully to make certain that any root initials (radicles) remain undamaged.

Artificial stratification lengthens the period in which these more difficult seeds can be grown. It is especially useful as it allows sowing to take place in the spring or in early autumn which produces a strong seedling before the winter. It does not always work, however, or sometimes only partially, so if results are poor keep the seed pan or leave the seed undisturbed in the soil so that it gets the benefit of the following natural winter.

One other reason for the poor germination of some seeds is that they only germinate in the wild after being subjected to some form of physical injury. This breaks down their hard seedcoat and allows moisture to penetrate into the seed inside. It may involve simple weathering, soil cultivation or even being passed through the digestive system of birds.

The wild flowers known to our parents and grandparents are becoming increasingly hard to find, but here cuckooflower and marsh-marigold still grow in an unspoilt meadow.

The process can take several weeks, months, or even years after the seed is shed and it is the main reason why some large seeds with hard coats often germinate so poorly. Damaging the seed coat, or scarifying as it is called, will help germination. Two garden plants which respond to such treatment are lupins and sweet peas.

A number of tough-coated and often large-seeded wild flowers will germinate much better after being scarified. They include meadow and dove's-foot crane's-bill and several members of the pea family including sainfoin, kidney vetch and the clovers. The best method of scarifying is to rub the seed between two sheets of medium-grade glass paper for several minutes until the seed coat looks well scraped or, in some cases, changes colour. Do not damage the seed embryo by over-enthusiasm and always sow it as soon as possible into a well-watered seedbed, pot or seed tray.

◆ DIRECT SOWING ◆

This is the easiest and most straightforward way of raising wild flowers and is the only practicable way of establishing a flowering mini-meadow. With wild flowers grown in a mixed border, or for a wild garden, results with many species can be less certain and will involve a favourable combination of site and soil conditions.

However, annuals like cornflower, corncockle, the chamomiles, corn marigold and field poppy, respond well to direct sowing and, with the right after-care, most of these should self-seed themselves and continue to give colour for year after year. Other wild flowers which will usually succeed from sowing where they are to flower include the biennials foxglove and mullein and perennials like ragged-robin, yarrow and oxeye daisy.

The best time of year to sow direct is either in early spring or late summer and early autumn, when the soil is still warm and germination and seedling establishment consequently rapid. This also allows the whole summer for thorough preparation of the seedbed and the elimination of weeds.

Most annual wild flowers will grow sturdy seedlings from an autumn sowing and stand through the hardest winter weather, especially if the soil is well-drained. If an autumn sowing is followed by a second in spring, the batches will flower in succession and give a longer period of display. Corn marigold is one annual which normally germinates in the wild in spring and might not survive an autumn sowing. For this reason, except in a protected situation, it might fail to regenerate naturally and need re-sowing every spring.

The preparation for spring sowing is best carried out during the previous autumn, which gives time for thorough digging and for the soil to settle during the winter. It also encourages an all-important frost tilth (a finely broken-up soil surface) to form on clay soils and this is especially important to help obtain the fine surface needed for sowing a mini-meadow. Do not sow seeds too early in spring but wait until you can get on to the soil without taking large lumps of it off on your boots. The latest date to sow is about mid-May after this dry conditions can spoil germination and establishment.

Although nature's way is to scatter seeds at random on the soil surface, this is when they are set in abundance and if some fail to germinate it is of little consequence. When sowing from your expensively-bought seed packets, you will achieve better results from a properly prepared bed, with the seed sown in drills made with a stick or hoe. Sow in round or oval-shaped patches, with the drills in each patch running at angles to each other, to avoid the regimented appearance of straight rows.

Very fine seeds like foxglove, mullein and meadow saxifrage need only shallow drills and little or no cover. For larger seeds the old horticultural rule applies of covering them with soil to their own depth. The very large seeds of species like meadow crane's-bill and field scabious need to be covered with twice their depth of soil. After sowing fairly thinly, cover the drills carefully without disturbing the seeds and lightly firm the soil with the back of a rake. If the weather is dry water sparingly using a fine rose, but do not over-water or over-firm or the soil surface may cap and spoil germination.

Germination of the seeds will be quite rapid in the autumn, when the soil is moist and still warm, and many seedlings should appear within 10–14 days. In the colder soils of spring it might take twice as long. The seedlings will often appear at erratic intervals and large seeds often take longer to come through than smaller ones. During this time some weeds may grow and their control will be easier if they are sown in drills rather than broadcast. You might also need to keep off intruders like cats and birds by using black thread and pepper dust.

Once the seedlings are big enough to handle they will need to be thinned, with the ultimate spacing depending on the eventual height of the plants and their type of growth. Most perennials need thinning to a distance of about half their eventual height but annuals like corn marigold, corncockle and cornflower can be left quite a bit closer, which

means they help support each other without needing to be staked. Plants grown together in clumps or groups also help suppress, or eliminate competition from, weeds.

Thinning in two stages can help reduce the risk of losses and gaps caused by slugs and other predators, but make certain the final thinning is done before the plants start seriously to compete with each other. Slugs are particularly partial to the fleshy leaves of wild flowers such as the oxeye daisy and large-flowered evening-primrose. Under moist conditions these flowers might need protecting with slug pellets.

◆ PLANT RAISING ◆

◆ Outdoors

Although annual wild flowers are almost always best sown where they are to flower, for a number of perennials and biennials it is often better to sow them in an outdoor nursery bed for later transplanting. This allows sowing during the best time, the early autumn period, while using the winter to construct the final bed into which the seedlings are moved the following spring. The reverse of sowing in spring followed by planting in autumn can also apply.

Choose a sheltered part of your garden with good soil for the seedbed and in an area free of perennial weeds. Prepare it as thoroughly as you would any area used for seed sowing and rake a light dressing of superphosphate into the surface before sowing to encourage root growth. The addition of compost, coarse peat or bark will help maintain an open soil structure.

Sow the seed thinly in drills, allowing at least a foot between each for hoeing. Mark the rows carefully but as labels can easily be lost or fade, it is also a good idea to make a plan of the sowings, adding for your interest and future information the dates of sowing and germination.

After germination, you can either thin the seedlings and leave them where they are for later transplanting into their flowering quarters, or move them into an intermediate nursery bed. The main advantage of a double move is that it will give a bigger plant with an improved root system, better able to cope with the competition of a mixed border. Plants kept in a thinned seedbed will usually prove quite satisfactory for an entirely new wild flower garden.

However the seedlings are raised, the period after transplanting is quite critical. Some root damage is bound to occur when lifting, so it is best to avoid moving in the summer months when transpiration is high and moisture stress at its maximum. For the same reason, it is never a good idea to move plants in very windy weather.

Although wild flowers, like many other plants, can be moved during clement weather in the winter, the best times are a quiet day when ground conditions are suitable in spring or autumn. Plant in well-prepared soil into which a light dressing of a general fertilizer has been forked, firm the plants well and give a light watering to settle the roots. Further watering might be needed in a dry spring, or even sometimes in a very dry autumn, but the aim should be to establish the plants well before either the hot weather starts in summer or cold and frost comes in winter. Check all autumn-set plants in early spring and re-firm the soil if they have been lifted by severe frosty weather.

◆ Under glass

If you compare the amount of seed you buy in many wild flower packets with, for example, the more common varieties of bedding plants and vegetables, you might be disappointed at how much you get for your money. This is mainly because all wild flower seed has to be picked and processed by hand; production can therefore be difficult and expensive. Even though crops of wild flowers are now grown specifically for seed, some species are still quite scarce.

To get full value for money and be more certain of results, in many cases it is better to raise seedlings under glass and plant them out either into a nursery bed or straight into the border. This also gives more flexibility in time of sowing and planting, better protection for seedlings over winter and often a better plant for transplanting. Sowing in trays will also give better results for the expensive and choicer species like cowslip, oxlip and primrose and many finer seeds such as harebell, meadow saxifrage and foxglove.

Although in theory many wild flowers may be raised under glass or in a frame at almost any time of the year, the two best periods are generally late February to May and late August to November. This avoids the highest temperatures of summer, when seed germination is difficult, and the coldest period of winter, when heat will be needed to make them grow.

Choose a well-structured, open growing medium such as a peat based sowing compost or properly made John Innes and use *clean* pots or boxes – wild flowers are just as prone to damping-off (the collapse and death of seedlings caused by the attack of a parasitic fungus) and other seedling diseases as any other plant. Firm the compost lightly and water it evenly, using a can with a fine rose. Sow the seeds evenly over the surface, mixing very small seeds with dry silver sand to make sowing easier.

Small seeds, like meadow saxifrage or harebell, need only to be lightly pressed into the surface and not covered with soil or compost. Most other seeds need covering with their own depth of compost; very large seeds to twice their depth. After covering, firm the compost lightly and cover all the containers with either glass or newspaper to prevent loss of moisture.

Although most wild flower seeds germinate best at a temperature of 15–20°C (60–68°F), they will also grow satisfactorily at lower temperatures – though more slowly. Avoid keeping them too warm in the early spring, when the light can be poor, but keep very high temperatures down in summer with an additional cover of expanded polystyrene, of the type often used in packing domestic and electrical appliances.

Germination can be rapid in warm conditions and you should inspect the containers every day, turning over the glass or Correx to dry off any condensed moisture. Wild flowers often do not germinate or grow so regularly as most cultivated plants. To avoid the seedlings getting drawn (elongated), remove the cover once the first ones have come through and do not wait for any laggards. After germination, water sparingly with a fine rose and place the seedlings in a well-lit situation but protected from strong sunshine with a light cover until the seed leaves (cotyledons) have fully expanded.

Once the seedlings are big enough to handle they can be pricked out, either directly into a nursery bed outdoors or into 7cm (3in) pots, using peat-based or John Innes potting compost. Alternatively, prick out into boxes before potting; the plastic multi-plug type modules have given good results. When potting or transplanting, try to disturb the plant root system as little as possible.

Keep the seedlings adequately watered during their time in the pots or modules but avoid over-watering. Even moisture-loving species like purple-loosestrife will not tolerate an over-wet and airless compost at the young seedling stage. The rule should be to water thoroughly only when it is needed, rather than give a frequent dribble which merely wets the surface. A sure sign that plants need watering in a loamless compost is when they start to shrink away from the pot edge.

The great advantage of growing in pots rather than a nursery bed is that pots give a good root system which is almost completely undisturbed when planting. Provided that the plants are kept well-watered until they are established, it also allows planting at almost any time from spring to autumn.

Conventional liquid or solid feeding can produce a plant out of character and is generally not needed in the seedling stage. However, with plants kept for a long time, the long-term type of controlled release fertilizers now available have given good results and will help prevent plants starving before you plant in a late spring.

If you are keeping plants in pots over winter, remember that they are hardy – otherwise they would not have become established in the wild under our often rather erratic climatic conditions. They will not need any heat and will survive quite happily in a cold frame given plenty of air. Even in winter remember, however, that plants in frames can dry out; so inspect them regularly and give water if it is needed. Sinking the pots rim-deep is a good alternative in light, well-drained soil but can lead to rooting-through in a mild winter.

If the compost and containers you have used for sowing are kept in the same frame, after a winter cold spell you will often find that as the weather warms up there is a second germination of seedlings as a spring bonus. This is quite normal for wild flowers, which frequently germinate over quite a long period.

◆ SOWING A MINI-MEADOW ◆

Coupled with careful site preparation, the choice of the correct seed mixture and the way it is sown will have a considerable effect on the successful establishment of a flowering mini-meadow. The choice of the correct mixture is dealt with later (page 142–4), but there are a number available and, should you wish, you can also make up your own. Generally, however, it is best to buy from specialists who have the experience to choose the right sort of grasses to use with a wild flower mixture for different soil types.

The amount of seed recommended for a mini-meadow is considerably lower than for ordinary lawns, with the normal sowing rate reduced to about 4g ($\frac{1}{7}$oz) per square metre. This is because the aim is not to obtain a quick close-knit lawn but a much more open sward which gives the often slower growing wild flowers time to develop. Increasing the recommended rate will give a quicker cover of grass but only at the expense of the wild flowers. The lower rate also helps to compensate for the increased seed cost of the wild flowers and some of the more expensive grasses which are used. This lower rate of seed can, however, be quite hard to sow accurately, especially as the smaller seeds can separate out under windy conditions. Using a dry carrier such as fine sand, fine sawdust or finely ground barley meal at one part seed to five parts carrier will help bulk up the seed and make it easier to sow. Before sowing you should also mix the grasses and flower seeds thoroughly by hand.

Even sowing will be helped by first marking out the area with string in square metres or yards. Weigh out enough seed for one square, sow it and see what it looks like. This will act as a guide for the whole area and will be even more effective if mixed with a light-coloured seed carrier. An alternative is to use a marked-off plastic drinking cup or other container as a measure for the required amount of seed or seed plus carrier. Larger areas can be sown using a lawn fertilizer spreader, but either use a carrier or make certain that the machine keeps the seed well-mixed while it is being sown.

After sowing, lightly rake or brush over the surface so that the seed is covered with a thin layer of soil. For fine soils free of stones a metal or plastic spring-tine lawn rake is ideal. When sowing in spring, or at any time when the soil is dry, reduce the loss of moisture from the soil by treading the surface. Wear shoes rather than boots, the heels of which can leave deep impressions. An alternative is to firm the surface with a roller-type lawn mower with the blades set high. Applying water can help germination in dry weather but is best done lightly by hand or using lay-flat irrigation. Many lawn sprinklers produce too large a droplet for use after sowing and by producing a capped soil surface, can do more harm than good.

As with lawns, there is probably no best time to sow a flowering mini-meadow but the period from early-August to mid-September has several advantages. The soil is at its warmest at that time, thereby speeding germination and establishment and giving a reasonable cover of the soil before winter. Any wild flowers needing winter cold treatment will germinate in the following spring and soon catch up with the rest – another reason for not sowing too thickly.

Next to late summer/early autumn, the best time to sow is from late March to early May when the soil starts to warm up but is usually still moist. Germination in spring will, however, be slower and this gives more time for annual weeds to grow and for seed to be plundered by birds. After early May, you run the risk of coming into a period of drought, when sun and wind can dry out the seedbed.

♦ BUYING WILD FLOWER SEED ♦
AND PLANTS

In the past it was common to dig up a clump of cowslips, primroses or bluebells and transport them into cottage gardens. This was not too damaging while there were plenty of wild flowers available and may have helped their survival in some areas. Today the situation has changed. Years of depredation and loss of habitats means that every naturally-sited wild flower is precious. Those remaining are there to be enjoyed and not disturbed – not even, some would say, by picking flowers or harvesting seed.

Furthermore, under the Wildlife and Conservation Act of 1981 there is a list of fully protected scheduled plants, recently increased (see page 148–50), which may under no circumstances be removed from the countryside. Under the same act it is also an offence to uproot *any* wild plant unless you are an authorised person or have the authority of the landowner. Technically, this almost certainly includes road verges.

Picking flowers or harvesting seed may seem harmless but for the scarce and more valuable species it can, in fact, help to hasten their disappearance. Although many are perennial, a number of wild flowers are not long-lived and rely on the growth of young seedlings to assist their regeneration. The cowslip, for example, will co-exist happily with sheep or other animals grazing on the village green but once the district council takes over with regular gang-mowing, the seeding cycle is lost and it quickly disappears. One obvious answer is to leave a rough strip around the edges which is only cut down two or three times a year. For annual wild flowers, re-seeding every year is, of course, their only way of survival. So although nobody will probably mind if you pick a few cornflowers or poppies for a flower display, if everybody does it a species can soon disappear.

Fortunately, there is no need to collect seeds yourself from the wild. Sales have increased to a point where most of the larger packet seed firms now offer a limited range of wild flower species and mixtures by mail order or through garden shops, while specialist suppliers sell a very much larger selection (see pages 152–5). Most of these seeds are now field-grown by specialist raisers or harvested from private wild flower collections.

If you are either too impatient for results to sow seed outdoors or have no facilities for raising under glass, wild flower plants are becoming easier to obtain. As with seed, some of the most popular are now stocked by many good plant centres but you will need to go to a specialist raiser to buy a fuller range of species. They are also available by mail order (see pages 152–5).

◆ SEED SAVING ◆

Once you have established a wild flower collection there is no reason why you should not harvest some of your own seed, either to extend your own planting or to pass it on to friends. Many wild flowers set seed quite rapidly after flowering but, unlike some cultivated plants, this can be extended for quite a long period. This will allow you to harvest the earliest seed to set but let the remainder fall, where the seedlings will either help fill out the existing clumps of flowers or can be thinned out later.

One point of caution, different species of the same genus of plants grown close together can cross-fertilize each other if grown close together. This includes the primula species cowslip, oxlip and primrose, and campanulas like harebell and both clustered and nettle-leaved bellflowers. They will also cross with related garden plants. Resulting seedlings will then be a mixture of each parent plant and some often rather indifferent in-between hybrids. Only take seed, therefore, from plants which are growing well away from others of the same wild or cultivated species.

Experience will show when wild flower seed is ready for harvesting but usually this is when the seed pods turn to brown from green. When really ripe, seeds from species like the cowslip, ragged-robin and harebell can be shaken out from the seed capsules in to a tray, open box, or bucket. For seeds with a protected seed pod or cluster, like the oxeye daisy, the knapweeds and salad burnet, either rub the seed between your finger and thumb into a container or pick the entire seed head and rub out later.

Low-growing plants such as lady's bedstraw, selfheal and common rest harrow can have entire stems removed with the seed pods, which often continue to ripen after they have been picked. When their seed is ripe, others like herb-robert, bird's-foot-trefoil and meadow crane's-bill have seed pods or capsules which burst explosively, firing the seed away from the plant. To make certain of saving the seed of these species, pick them before they are fully ripe and hang the stems upside down in a paper or linen bag. Never use polythene bags for either saving or storing seeds; they will only sweat inside and turn the contents mouldy.

Thereafter it is quite a simple matter to dry the seed by laying it out on a tray which is kept under cover or put in the sun, cleaning out any bits of pod or other plant debris and then sowing it as you would seed from a packet. In muggy, humid weather, cold air blown from a greenhouse or room heater will help seeds dry but under no circumstances try and speed up drying with warm air or by using an airing cupboard, which spoils germination. If you are going to keep the seed for sowing later, packet it in well marked and fastened envelopes and store in dry, cool conditions – such as an old country larder. Both greenhouses and the average small garden shed get too warm in summer to be ideal places for storing any type of seeds.

With a mixed bed of annuals it is often better to pick off the seed and re-sow it, rather than let the plants seed themselves. This will maintain the balance of flowers and prevent domination by the strongest species. Harvest each species as it ripens and once the latest has finished flowering, usually by September, remove all the plants together with any grass or other weeds. Fork over the ground thoroughly, firm it by treading, rake in a light application of a general fertilizer such as Growmore and sow the seed in drills (page 18); the re-sowing of corn marigold is best left until the following spring (page 17).

Having saved what can easily be a surprisingly large amount of seed, you might be tempted to help conserve the wild flowers by scattering some of it around the countryside. Although your impulse will be understandable and entirely honourable, resist it; you might do more harm than good.

Winter aconite

There are probably good reasons for the absence of certain species in some areas so trying to introduce them there is often unsuccessful but even should they establish, you could upset a delicate balance in the natural habitat. This could be responsible for an existing species disappearing altogether. Many areas also have their own subspecies or forms of plants developed to suit a particular set of conditions. By introducing a different form you could encourage hybrid seedlings and the original local type being lost.

Although most of the really disastrous introductions to a new environment concerns animals, such as rabbits and the grey squirrel, there are also several cases of land and water plants introduced to a foreign habitat getting out of control. Indian balsam and giant hogweed are two examples. So it is best to keep the wild flower seeds you have saved within the confines of your garden or those of your friends.

◆ OTHER MEANS OF PLANT ◆ PROPAGATION

Seed is by no means the only way that wild flowers spread themselves in nature. Runners, stolons (shoots from the plant root), underground roots and stems and natural plant division are all used as alternatives and for some this is often a more certain way of reproduction than seed. For example, the seed of sweet violet is often difficult to germinate well, even with stratification, but it will propagate from stem cuttings and runners quite easily. Rooted runners can be taken off the plants at almost any time after flowering from late spring to early autumn and either grown on in a cold frame, or direct-planted into a shady, moist spot in the garden.

To increase your stock of violets even further, divide the stems into cuttings about an inch long, each with a leaf joint. Fill a box or pot with seed-sowing compost and insert the cuttings just below the surface with the leaves left above it. Place in a cold frame or in the shadow of a north wall or fence and damp down in hot weather. Once rooted the young plants can either be planted or potted on to make a larger plant for setting out later. Other wild flowers can be rooted in a similar way.

Another type of cutting is from shoot tips; this is suitable for the cuckooflower, or lady's smock, which also can be difficult from seed. The cuttings are usually taken in late summer and placed in a propagating frame for rooting, before being potted and stood for the winter in a cold frame.

Basal cuttings can be taken from many perennial wild flowers including oxeye daisy, ragged-robin and small scabious. Young shoots 7–10cm (3–4in) long are taken from the base of well-established plants in spring, inserted to about half their depth into pots or boxes filled with propagating compost and placed in a cold frame. If taken carefully, some might already have some roots attached, but all should root quite quickly and can be potted singly to grow on, before being planted out in the border by late summer/early autumn.

The mulleins and other wild flowers that have fleshy roots can be propagated quite easily by root cuttings. Take sections of roots 2.5–5cm (1–2in) long in the autumn, give a shallow covering of propagating compost in trays or boxes and keep them free of frost over winter. By late spring they should have rooted and can be potted for planting in the autumn.

Many perennial wild flowers can be increased very easily by division, or splitting the clumps. The best time to do this is in the early autumn, which gives them time to settle before the winter. Some plants, for example, primroses will divide very well after they have finished flowering in spring. It is best to lift the whole clump, rather than try to slice off a section, and split it into two or more pieces before re-planting. Some plants will come apart easily by hand but others forming large clumps, such as oxeye daisy, might need two forks back-to-back to split them. Only use the young, outside pieces for planting back and throw away the woody centres.

The stock of many bulbous wild flowers can be increased by lifting and splitting the clumps into separate bulbs at the appropriate time. This can also maintain flower size by preventing over-crowding. Dig up and split clumps of wild daffodil, ramsons (wild garlic) and bluebells as soon as the tops have died down and either replant immediately, or dry off the bulbs and store them until planting in the autumn. The smaller, early-flowering bulbs such as the snowdrop and winter aconite often seem to split and transplant best immediately after they have finished flowering but before, rather than after, their tops have died down.

As a rough guide, all the bulbs should be planted in the soil to about three times their depth. Less than this and they can lift their way to the surface or, especially under fallen leaves, be scratched up by birds. Mice and other small rodents also eat the bulbs of small species, so look for tell-tale holes near where your bulbs have been planted and take appropriate steps.

◆ THE AFTER-CARE OF WILD FLOWERS ◆

As with all garden plants, to be seen at their best wild flowers need looking after. This applies equally whether you grow them in a mixed border or in a separate wild garden. Otherwise, although natural survivors, the balance of form and colour which you have tried to create will be lost as some survive rather more successfully than others.

The work involved, however, need not be arduous and, as with all forms of gardening, will often depend on the right steps being taken at

the right time. In a windy garden, for example, staking might be needed for some of the taller plants, especially in the first year or two before they are fully established. Use twiggy sticks 7–10cm (3–4in) shorter than the eventual height of the plant when the shoots are no more than half grown. This will give support that is not obtrusive and avoid any last-minute panics with unsightly canes and string.

Annual weeds may also be a problem in the early years and must be controlled. Later, if you have planned a good selection, the plant clumps should suppress most of them. A mulch of bark chippings will also help keep down the weeds, in addition to maintaining moisture, but make sure the bark does not smother some of the lower growing species.

Despite thorough preparation of a border, pernicious perennial weeds which grow up and often twine through the plants can still be a problem. This is because some of them like bindweed and mare's-tail often send roots way below the depth of normal digging. Given patience and persistence they can be dealt with successfully by painting the growing tips with the gel form of Tumbleweed or by squirting on hormone-type weedkiller from a carefully directed squeezy bottle. Take great care, however, to see that neither material comes into contact with your plants.

Unless the soil is very poor, when a light dressing of Growmore can be given each spring, there should be little need to feed wild flowers. In fact, to over-feed with high nitrogen type fertilizers can produce plants out of character, spoil the balance of the border and produce an excessive amount of growth. An application of sulphate of potash and bonemeal will, however, help re-establishment when splitting plants and re-planting them.

The balance of flowers in a border or wild flower garden will only be maintained by regular dead-heading. As mentioned under seed-saving (page 24), many wild plants are very prolific and will quickly over-crowd each other if all the seed they produce is shed and germinates. To take off unwanted heads as they finish flowering not only improves the appearance of a garden and helps prolong flowering, but saves a great deal of unnecessary work in thinning out the seedlings later. Like many other garden plants, keeping wild flowers free of seedheads can also help give a second flush of flowers.

Like any other plants, wild flowers are by no means immune to pests and diseases. In the wild you will often see fat-hen and its relative good-King-Henry smothered in black aphids, groundsel attacked by the fungus disease causing rust and many wild plants covered with mildew in autumn. Whether you want to control them, however, is entirely up to you. If you regard wild flowers as normal garden plants, you might wish to also prevent them from being damaged by the same sorts of pests and diseases. The worst of these are normally various types of aphids such as blackfly and greenfly, red spider, slugs and snails, assorted caterpillars and, occasionally, whitefly.

Many pests are worse in some years than others and a number have their own favourite plants. Relatively safe insecticides are available to deal with them; derris is one which will control a wide range of pests but even this is harmful to fish, so should not be sprayed near ponds or until evening when there is less risk of damage to bees. Used carefully, metaldehyde pellets will deal safely with slugs and snails and all modern formulations now contain an animal repellent.

The worst diseases are mildew, usually worst in the autumn, and botrytis, or grey mould, which can damage young plants in the border and during propagation. Benlate will control both these diseases if applied once the first signs appear, but be careful to keep excessive amounts from the soil as it is disliked by worms.

A pest to us can be somebody else's dinner. In a true wild garden, where you are trying to establish a natural ecological balance, you might well prefer to eschew all fungicides and insecticides and let nature take its course. This it will do, but though natural predators may be plentiful in a country garden even this might depend on where you live. The natural reservoir in the prairie-farm areas of eastern England, for example, is still low following a period of 'if it moves, spray it' – though, thankfully, this is now changing.

For the majority of town gardeners the natural balance of pest to predator will also take time to establish. There are bound to be a number of cats to feed into the equation; as recent studies have shown, these can have a considerable adverse effect on bird predator populations in an average suburb. Hedgehogs, invaluable for controlling slugs, snails and beetles, also take time to establish a population in a new housing estate. Then, provided there is plenty of developing cover, like urban foxes they seem to take quite happily to civilisation.

So until a balance is struck, you may be forced into a certain amount of judicious spraying. If you are careful with what you use, only spray in the very early morning or late in the evening when bees and butterflies are less active, avoid spraying open flowers and, above all, give any ladybirds present a chance to deal with an outbreak of greenfly, you will lessen the risk to the environment and probably be surprised at how few chemicals eventually you will need.

Even though 'pests' will cause some damage on your plants, in a wild garden you might still think it worth maintaining a level of them to help encourage birds and other natural predators. Wild flowers are also frequently hosts for a number of caterpillars, which eventually turn into moths or butterflies. Here you might have to face the choice between saving your plant and whatever is eating it. The great mullein for example, worth a place in any garden, is often severely damaged by the caterpillars of the beautiful mullein moth. The plant is seldom killed, however, and it would take a very hard-hearted gardener indeed to want to spray it.

• MAINTENANCE OF A MINI-MEADOW •

In the first year after sowing a flowering meadow needs looking after more carefully than in subsequent years. Most of the first seedlings to germinate will be some of the natural annual weeds like chickweed, shepherd's-purse and groundsel. As with any ordinary lawn, these do not matter very much. They will soon disappear following the first clipping and even give some shelter to the more delicate seedlings germinating later.

Perennial weeds, especially coarse grasses like couch are, however, much more damaging and once allowed to establish will prove almost impossible to eradicate. Some may come from pieces of root left near the surface during pre-sowing cultivations; these will often pull out quite easily by hand but re-firm down any soil disturbed in removing them. An alternative method is to wipe on Tumbleweed gel.

When the young sward has reached a height of about 10cm (4in), it can be given its first cut, setting the mower blade at a height of about 5cm (2in). Roll the soil lightly before cutting if the soil is moist and there is any danger of young seedlings being up-rooted by the mower. A rotary type machine will usually give a better cut at this height than a cylinder mower. A cut to the same height at about monthly intervals for the first season will ensure air, light and moisture reach all the developing seedlings. Remove all the clippings which will otherwise tend to stifle the growth of some of the finer flowers and, as they rot, help build up too high a level of soil fertility. This repeated cutting should encourage the establishment of the relatively slow-growing wild flowers and prevent the ascendancy of the stronger growing grasses. At all costs, avoid the build-up of a canopy of grass above the flowers below.

By the end of the first season, the young mini-meadow should contain a mixture of flowers at various stages of development with prostrate (low growing) and the less-vigorous grasses. Some of the more vigorous wild flowers like black medick, common sorrel, kidney vetch, oxeye daisy, ribwort plantain, selfheal and yarrow will already be quite large plants. Other slower growing types like the common and greater knapweed, field scabious, hoary plantain, lady's bedstraw, rough hawkbit, small scabious and several others will be still quite small. If you sowed in spring, some plants, including cowslip, harebell and meadow crane's-bill might not come through until experiencing a cold spell during the first winter.

In the second year, the wild flowers grow, mature, flower and set their seed. Ideally, the sward should not be cut until all this seed is shed but this can be quite late for some species. To keep it looking reasonably tidy and to prevent the grasses over-growing the flowers, a compromise of giving the first cut in April, followed by a second in July after the early seed has been shed and a third late in the season to tidy it up for winter usually achieves a reasonable balance.

In subsequent years you will see variations in the proportions of the various plant species in your mini-meadow. As it matures the balance inevitably will favour those most suitable for your soil type and climatic conditions – this is merely a mirror-image of what has always happened in nature. However, your sward will be encouraged to remain species-rich if your cutting and management is timed to fit in with the main flowering periods. Summer-flowering species, for example, are often especially attractive to butterflies and bees and they will flower at their best if given two early clippings and another much later in autumn, after all the self-set seed has been shed. Flowering bulbs in the sward are one example where cutting must be delayed until the foliage has completely died down, if they are to spread successfully and continue to flower every year.

After the first year a standard cutting height of 7cm (3in) will usually achieve a good balance of species, through which a closer-mown path can be cut for walking and to admire the flowers. The grass should always be removed after cutting (see page 13). This can be made easier by leaving it to dry before it is removed, when the species-rich hay will be appreciated by pet rabbits or any other grass eating small animals you might keep. Such hay can be stored for the winter in a dry shed or lean-to but make sure it is thoroughly dried and not allowed to get damp.

Fertilizers will have a similar effect to leaving clippings to rot on the surface of a mini-meadow and because they will only encourage vigorous grasses at the expense of the flowers in the sward, should be avoided. If you really want a traditional green striped grass strip, you should concentrate on your ornamental lawn.

Perennial broad-leaved weeds like thistle, dock and ragwort, as well as coarser grasses such as couch and Yorkshire-fog, can dominate a flowering sward unless controlled. Deal with them individually as they appear by hand removal or using Tumbleweed gel. Overall spray or watering-can applications of hormone-type weedkillers should never, of course, be used on a mini-meadow at any time.

ESTABLISHING WILD FLOWERS IN THE GARDEN

• THE RIGHT PLANT IN THE RIGHT PLACE •

A weed is really what we want to make it, be it a wild plant or a plant that has escaped from cultivation. Deciding the difference between a weed and a wild flower worth growing in the garden is largely a matter for personal choice – together with the space available. Few gardeners, for example, would want to give garden space to really invasive plants like the field and hedge bindweed, but both can have a colourful place in the right situation. Others, like the great mullein, alexanders and teasel, make a striking display given enough room but might be too tall or spreading for a small garden.

The other approach, and one which is sometimes very tempting, is merely to let nature run its course and take what comes. A few garden owners have in this way abandoned all attempts at cultivation and garden management and apparently live quite happily surrounded by a wilderness – though whether this is inspired by their love for ecology or more by natural indolence probably only they can say.

A really satisfactory display of garden wild flowers therefore needs a certain amount of planning to ensure a blend of sizes, shapes, colour and flowering seasons. This will help fit them into mixed borders but is even more essential for a complete wild flower garden, if each plant is to be seen at its best and stand a reasonable chance of survival.

As with planting any garden, the main points you need to take into account when planning for wild flowers include knowing their size and shape, the type and colours of the plants and, lastly your own personal preferences.

The size of your garden will obviously largely determine both the number and, to some extent, the type of wild flowers you can grow. Experience will show exactly how much room each species will need, but in general it is better to grow them in a clump of at least three or four together rather than as single specimens. This type of planting usually

Most gardens contain a patch of grass which can be used to grow some sun-loving meadow flowers. This display includes hogweed, red clover, meadow buttercup and cat's-ear.

gives greater flowering impact and is generally easier to manage. Like other garden plants, heights need to be graded with the tallest at the back of the border, or in the middle of an island bed, and the shortest in the front. Always allow for the extra centimetres that plants will grow in good garden soil and conditions and in a wet season.

Many wild flowers are tolerant of a range of soils especially when grown free of competition from grass or other competitive plants, but some have definite preferences. Those plants which originate from chalky downlands like the harebell, rock-rose and wild thyme grow well in alkaline soils whilst acid soils, which are often sandy, will see an abundance of sorrel, the native heather and wild pansy.

A simple soil test will establish whether your garden is acid or alkaline but you will also get a good indication from the type of garden plants growing successfully in the area – rhododendrons, azaleas and camelias, for example, being notorious calcifuges, or lime-haters. Although measures can be taken to make the soil more acid or alkaline to suit different plants, this can be expensive and time-consuming and is rarely permanently successful. To grow what is more native to your type of soil and area seems more within the spirit of wild flower gardening and will, in any case, give you a wide range to choose from.

The depth of your soil will also determine how successfully you are with some wild flowers. Although a number grow quite happily in dry, thin soils and in full sun, others are more moisture loving and either need growing in a wet situation or under shade where they are less likely to dry out in summer. Here again, study the natural vegetation or take a look with a spade to inspect the depth of soil and the freedom of drainage, which will indicate whether the site is likely to be basically wet or dry. Obviously climate will also come into this, with some plants showing a preference for the wetter western part of the country over the much drier eastern counties.

Like garden plants, wild flowers have their preferences for site and situation. Some of this is coupled with a need for moisture but there are also considerable differences in their tolerance to shade or sunshine. A number of woodland and edge-of-wood plants flower happily in full sun in spring but need shade in the heat of summer whilst some climbers, traveller's-joy or wild clematis is one example, grow best with their roots in the shade but with the flowers clambering out into the full sun.

In a garden with surrounding buildings and given a framework of trees and shrubs, it should not be too difficult to select the right area for the right plants, or provide it if it is not there already. Remember, too, that even plants which thrive in full sun seldom need this for every hour of daylight – even should our climate provide it! An open, southerly aspect is normally sufficient and the lower growing sun-lovers will mostly tolerate a fair amount of light dappled shade from nearby deciduous trees in summer. Taller growing species, on the other hand, need planting as far away from shade or fences and walls as possible if

A border in the award-winning Gale's Honey Bee Garden at Chelsea Flower Show (1988) demonstrates how wild flowers can be grown alongside cultivated plants to great effect.

they are to grow without staking and the risk of them falling over the shorter plants in front.

The question of choosing plants to associate together to give a good blend of colour and a long flowering season is largely personal preference. Obviously if you are growing an entirely wild garden you need a blend to give flower continuously from spring to autumn. You will also be helped by the fact that, given good cultivation and with careful dead-heading, plants often flower much longer in the garden than they do in the wild.

For wild flowers grown with other plants you might, however, prefer to be more selective and concentrate on those which add something special at certain times of the year. Cowslips in an open border or in clumps in the grass, primroses on a sunny bank and sweet violets in a shady corner are all worth a special place in any garden to help brighten up the spring. Late on in the summer is another time when other flowers like the blue scabious, yellow elecampane, pink musk mallow and, for a moist situation, the pale-pink hemp-agrimony, the slender, purple-loosestrife and several others which help bring interest to borders short of colour from traditional garden plants.

Wild flowers can also give a slightly different colour dimension to a garden. Many of the sometimes rather strident reds, pinks and blues seen in gardens nowadays either originate from warmer climates, where colours are mostly brighter, or have been hybridised by seedsmen seeking something different. The colours of our native flowers are generally more subtle and restrained, which is surely part of their charm. The old cottage gardens also showed that if enough of them are grown together, few colours actually clash.

At the same time, should you want to fit them into the existing basic colour scheme of a border or have strong preferences, you could choose a succession of plants to give you flowers of a single colour through from spring to autumn.

Plants like bluebell, germander speedwell, lesser periwinkle, columbine or the native aquilegia, harebell, Jacob's-ladder, nettle-leaved bellflower and viper's-bugloss would give a good succession of blues; for yellow, use primrose, cowslip, common bird's-foot-trefoil, greater celandine, great and hoary mullein, lady's bedstraw, common St John's-wort and common evening-primrose; for pink, herb-robert, cuckooflower or lady's smock, Cheddar pink, foxglove, common restharrow, sainfoin, hemp-agrimony and soapwort.

As you get to know wild flowers better, you will come to realise that there are many more similar colour combinations and find how they can fit into your own garden philosophy and situation. As well as the flowers, there are also many different leaf shapes and plant forms to provide a contrast with both wild and conventional garden plants. Grasses, ferns, herbs and many other plants can all be used to give a blend suitable for any garden from the largest to the smallest.

As with any form of gardening, it is important to know something about the plants you are trying to grow as well as having fun growing them. If they should then prove unsatisfactory or turn out to be the wrong plants in the wrong place, cut your losses and try again. That really is one of the great benefits of wild flowers; they are not hard to grow, are fairly tolerant of treatment and not expensive. Growing them opens up a multitude of possibilities and a whole new interest to the garden.

◆ MIXED GARDENS ◆

Most gardeners will start growing wild flowers by planting the occasional favourite plant into a conventional type of border. Indeed, there must be very few gardens at all which do not already include some representatives from the wild, like bluebell, foxglove, sweet violet, wild pansy, primrose and cowslip – even if they are only some of the more modern hybridised 'improved' forms.

This is not to decry plants like coloured cowslips and primroses. They make very good and colourful indoor winter or spring pot plants and are often ideal for places in the garden such as patio tubs and boxes. In the mixed border, however, it is generally better to stick to one or the other. This will avoid too glaring a contrast between the old and the new and also prevent cross-pollination, generally followed by the production of a number of usually inferior hybridised seedlings.

A mixed border is an ideal way to start growing wild flowers. A few clumps of some of the most showy species will not only help convince you of their many merits, but also show how easily they fit in with normal garden management. You may then also be surprised to find that far from looking 'wild', when free of the intense competition in nature, many native plants behave much like any others. Yet at the same time they can provide a contrast of forms to the often more rigid-growing imported and exotic species.

Yellow archangel

Nevertheless, in a mixed planting you will want to grow plants which add something to the border and are not there as mere curiosities. The following is a 'top ten' short list of good, summer-flowering perennials chosen to give a range of colours in either sunny or shady situations and which will mix happily with other garden plants. Further details of each plant are given on pages 69–132.

◆ **Sunny border**

Common evening primrose*   yellow, sweet-scented
Field scabious   mauve, tolerant of poor soil and drought
Great mullein*   yellow, attractive to bees
Jacob's-ladder   blue, May–July, a popular garden plant
Meadow crane's-bill   useful for foliage and flowers
Musk mallow   rose-pink, large-flowered and bushy
Nettle-leaved bellflower   blue, can be invasive
Oxeye daisy   white, more free-flowering and less vigorous than the related 'Esther Read'
Purple-loosestrife   Purple, best in a moist soil or marsh
Ragged-robin   pinky-red, best in damp soil, attracts butt...

◆ **Slightly shaded border**

Bluebell   blue, best planted around shrubs and trees
Bugle   blue, purple-green foliage, good ground cover
Columbine   purplish-blue, attractive spring foliage
Dark mullein*   yellow with purple centres, also grows
Devil's-bit scabious   mauve, chalky soils preferred
Foxglove*   purple, prefers fertile, slightly acid soils
Red campion   rose-red, useful for flower arrangement
Tufted vetch   blue-purple, colourful climber
Water avens   purple-orange, needs moist soil
Yellow archangel   yellow, good ground cover

* biennial plants but will self-seed readily once establish
the areas around the plants are kept free of grass and unwanted pla...

These selections will give you a basis for your mixed border but they are by no means exhaustive. Some dwarf species like wild pansy, for example, can be most effective for under-planting roses or some of the taller shrubs. This delightful native flower with its tricolour face, often known as heart's-ease, will flower for much of the spring, summer and autumn, and sometimes even through a mild winter. To keep it flowering, like cultivated pansies, it needs dead-heading but a few seed pods left to ripen will ensure it regenerates by self-seeding. To keep it true, make sure that it does not cross-pollinate with pansies or violas.

The delicate yellow-green flowers and downy green foliage of the slightly taller lady's-mantle can look most effective as a ground cover under standard roses, or in a mixed bed with semi-dwarf conifers. It is also a particularly useful plant for flower arrangers, fresh or dried. In fertile soils, however, it can become invasive by both self-seeding and vegetative propagation, smothering other small plants nearby. Always remove the flowers before they set seeds, therefore, and thin out the plants regularly.

Another useful climbing plant for a sunny spot is the narrow-leaved everlasting-pea. Unlike its cultivated annual cousins, which came originally from southern Europe, once planted this native perennial will come up every year to brighten a sunny corner with a mass of purple-red flowers from June–August. It will climb over anything which will support it; unfortunately, it has no scent.

◆ WILD GARDENS IN THE SUN ◆

The next step from planting wild flowers in a mixed border, or using them in combination with cultivated plants, is to establish separate wild flower beds or gardens. This allows you to experiment with a much wider range of native plants and even establish a type of mini-countryside in your garden. To biologists this is known as an ecosystem and means that eventually the wild flowers will help a type of wildlife reserve to become established, where butterflies, bees and other beneficial insects and animals like frogs and hedgehogs will flourish.

For planting a garden in the sun you can use many of the same plants as in a mixed border, but you should also have room for some which may not be so spectacular in flower yet are worth growing for the sake of interest.

A range of your most favourite wild flowers can be selected to give height and colour over a long flowering season. Most of the plants should be perennials, so will die down in winter to reappear in spring. Annuals such as field poppy, corn marigold, cornflower and wild pansy will usually produce plenty of self-sown seedlings every year, providing the area is kept free of grass and unwanted plants. Some of the species chosen should be particularly attractive to bees and butterflies.

When choosing a range of plants for a sunny or slightly shaded site, teasel is an excellent plant to include. This can grow up to 1.8m (6ft) tall and although the mauve flowers are not especially striking, they are attractive to bees whilst later the seeds are taken by seed-eating birds. Teasels are biennial, but self-seed easily, and the stalks remain to give a feature in the garden over winter. They can also be used for dried flower arrangements.

Another interesting plant is wild strawberry. This native species of the popular fruit makes a good ground cover or front-of-the-border plant, where it gives a mass of white flowers in April–July followed by fruits in June–August. The fruits are very attractive to a number of birds and although more tedious to pick, they are far sweeter and more flavoursome than their larger, cultivated cousins. The sweet, alpine strawberry is a fairly close relative.

As with a mixed garden border, to be seen at its best a wild flower garden needs to have most plants growing in clumps rather than as single specimens. This means planting them in groups of at least three or four, stopping them from competing with each other by regular dead-heading and restricting their vegetative spread.

A few sun-loving wild flowers also grow well as single dot plants, particularly to give spots of height or brighter colour to a garden. Plants that are particularly suitable for this are the foxglove, the great mullein, the brilliant blue viper's-bugloss, an outstanding plant for many nectar-loving insects, and feverfew, which gives a mass of white flowers from a single plant but if allowed to seed will soon spread all over the garden.

A really sunny corner of the garden is also an ideal spot in which to establish a border entirely composed of annual wild flowers. If the site is also free-draining and not too fertile it will help to stop them growing too strongly and flopping over in wet and windy weather. In this collection you can use many of the one-time 'weeds' of cultivated land, which, since the universal use of modern weedkillers, are now increasingly hard to find.

The purple corncockle, blue cornflower and buttercup-yellow corn marigold are now almost naturally extinct but were once widely seen in crops of cereals. Of the three, corn marigold is perhaps the best garden plant with a flowering season that can last from June until at least the end of October. It is also taller and much brighter than some varieties of the pot marigold, or calendula, which is not a native.

The rather harsher yellow of charlock, another one-time weed of corn, may not be to the taste of everyone but it grows very quickly and flowers early in the year from April until June. Do not sow it, however, if you are using the site of a previous vegetable patch with a history of club root disease, to which, as a member of the cruciferae family, it is very susceptible.

Other annual wild flowers well worth growing in your collection include the purple-flowered common fumitory, field forget-me-not, which flowers right through spring and summer, scarlet pimpernel, still

Wild strawberry

fairly common in waste places, corn chamomile, scentless mayweed and white campion, actually a short-lived perennial but best treated as an annual. All these, with most of the others, will normally self-seed themselves once they have become established, as long as the area is kept free from grass and unwanted plants. To stop the strongest taking over from the weakest, keep all the seedlings within their original groups and even though a number will germinate in the autumn, leave any thinning or transplanting necessary until spring to allow for winter losses. Thinnings can be used as a valuable source of plant material for species which can be effectively used in other parts of the garden.

◆ WILD FLOWERS IN SHADY AND ◆ WOODY SITES

A shady garden is where a number of wild flowers really come into their own. Of all the problems set by gardeners, one of the most common is 'what can I grow under trees or in a sunless situation?' One answer is a range of native wild flowers – a number of which have become acclimatised to growing in quite poor light and little sunshine.

The first group of these flower in early spring before the leaves come on the trees. Once they have finished flowering they are quite happy to spend a summer dormant period under a thick canopy of foliage. Early bulbs like winter aconite, snowdrop and the wild daffodil come into this group; other early bloomers include the yellow lesser celandine, a good carpet for the edge of a wood, the white flowered wood sorrel, primrose and the pale-blue common dog-violet – which although scentless, surely deserves a better name.

The next group are those which normally grow in the sun but will tolerate a fair amount of shade from trees or buildings, provided that it is not too gloomy. Some of these plants have already been listed in the section on mixed borders. Other good plants include Solomon's-seal, now rarely found in the wild, the purple-red betony, also quite hard to find, perforate St John's-wort, perhaps the best of several native species, germander speedwell, especially for growing up a shady bank and lesser periwinkle, not a true native but now widely naturalised throughout the country and a very old garden plant.

The real shade lovers come from deciduous woodlands and therefore need a normally damp situation with plenty of leaf mould or peat worked into the soil to simulate their natural conditions. Many are at their best in spring, when they will brighten up any gloomy part of the garden. These include the early-flowering wood anemone, wood spurge with greeny-yellow flowers and foliage to brighten up the darkest corner, the green hellebore and the related stinking hellebore, virtually evergreen and which will flower from December in a mild winter, and lungwort with pink flowers and spotted foliage giving good ground cover throughout the summer.

Wood crane's-bill is a delightful member of a popular family which thrives in shady conditions. The purple-pink flowers mainly come out in June–July but some blooms will continue to show until early autumn. It should establish easily but prefers a slightly acid soil. Slightly earlier to flower is woodruff, which needs heavy shade for the white star-like flowers and bright green leaves to be seen at their best. Flowering at about the same time is lily-of-the-valley, which needs a well-drained sandy soil to be seen at its best and does not like too much competition from other plants.

For length of attraction in a shady spot, there can be few plants to beat lords-and-ladies, often also called cuckoo-pint. This starts with the leaves appearing in mid-winter, followed by the unusual and decorative flowers in April to May, rather like a green-flowered arum lily, succeeded by orange berries in August. These berries are poisonous and this plant is probably best not grown in a garden with young children who might be attracted to them.

As a contrast to flowers and other foliage, a number of ferns thrive in shade and although many will establish best with plenty of moisture, once established they can be very tolerant to dry conditions. Hart's tongue, maidenhair and the male-fern provide three very contrasting native forms from this very large group; all grow best either in crevices or at the base of a north-facing wall.

Lastly, the native fragrant honeysuckle, or woodbine, is ideal to plant in shade to grow over the trees, fences or walls so that it flowers in the sun. This copies its natural habit, also shared by traveller's-joy, of growing inside a wood but clambering through to the light to flower. Honeysuckle is very tolerant of dry, poor conditions but if the soil is more fertile and growth too vigorous, keep it under control by annual trimming.

◆ WILD FLOWERS FOR WET SPOTS ◆ AND PONDS

If our forefathers were to return to the countryside today, one thing they would notice, apart from the lack of trees and hedges, is how dry it is compared to their day. Many of their ditches and ponds have been filled in and, with the exception of the occasional floods, water levels generally are now much lower.

Much of this is due to years of better agricultural land drainage, coupled with the straightening and dredging of streams and rivers. Of course, there is also a much higher level of water extraction, both to meet the needs of industry and those of a better plumbed population.

Not only are river levels generally lower, but many marshes are now drained and the old, traditional water meadows are virtually non-existent.

The water meadows were the natural home of many marsh and wet-loving wild flowers, which in consequence have become much harder to find. Although the construction of new reservoirs and the lakes left after gravel extraction has actually increased the area of standing water in some areas of the countryside, most of these are in great demand for popular activities like water sports and fishing. Relatively few, in fact, have been reserved for the preservation of natural, undisturbed wild life, though the number is slowly increasing.

In the meantime, we can help preserve many of these most beautiful moisture-loving plants in our gardens. Few gardens can be without their wet spots, even if it is only an area of poor drainage left by the disturbance of builders. If the soil is naturally wet and heavy, many moisture-lovers will also succeed in a normal flower border, mixed with other plants.

It is not difficult to make a wet place, or mini-marsh, in even the lightest and best drained garden soils. Simply take out the soil to about 30cm (12in) deep, and bury a sheet of thick polythene slightly bigger than the area you wish to plant and with the edges turned upwards. A discarded pond liner or even old flooring vinyl can be used as an alternative. Replace the top soil mixed with a liberal amount of sedge peat, bark or well-rotted compost, but not fresh manure, and be liberal with the hosepipe in very dry weather until the plants are well-established.

Native marsh plants which will thrive in such a situation include the lovely cream, late-flowering meadowsweet, the pale lilac cuckooflower, or lady's smock, rose-red and free-flowering ragged-robin, pale-pink common valerian and the yellow and purple-loosestrife – the latter surely one of the most stately wild flowers for the garden. A garden mini-marsh can also be the home of a number of native grass-like or grass wetland plants. Species like the common spike-rush and the soft rush, the common, hairy and lesser pond sedges and some water-loving grasses such as brown bent, meadow foxtail and purple moor-grass are all most attractive and will become home for a range of wildlife. They will, however, need keeping moist throughout the summer.

An area naturally wet and poorly drained in a large garden, which you do not want to drain and cultivate, will make a very attractive wetland meadow. Here you can first sow a wetland grass and wild flower mixture then once the sward is established, plant sedges, rushes and other moisture-loving flowering plants into it. Maintenance will consist of cutting once or twice a year when it is dry enough to get on the surface.

An extended pond margin is an ideal place in which to create a mini-marsh. To do this, when excavating and building the pond buy an over-sized liner, butyl rubber is best, and take the edges out well beyond the border of it to come up just below the soil surface. This area can then be used for plants that like to live in very boggy conditions and others which spread into the water. Good species include yellow iris, the long-flowering, blue veronica commonly known as brooklime and pink water avens.

Ponds as such can be a difficult feature to fit satisfactorily into a garden. So many are set in the middle of an open, manicured lawn with hard, rectangular edges, topped by a gently playing fountain and filled with little more interesting than a clutch of rather bored and overfed goldfish. This can suit the scale of a stately home, but rarely harmonises well with the average garden. It also gives little protection for wild life, for which ponds are a natural haven.

To be really successful, ponds need to be rather secretive, quiet places which blend in naturally with the rest of the garden. This often means leading gradually from the sunny border through semi-shade and the mini-marsh to the pond itself. A really well-established and sited pond will usually appear, in fact, to be a quite normal feature of the landscape – as though nature would have put one there in the first place, but somehow had not got around to it. Perfect examples of this are seen in many of the lakes designed for stately homes by the great landscape gardeners, but the principle can apply equally to a small garden pond.

Pond plants themselves are divided into several categories, leading from the margins to the centre of the water. You will see this in any existing pond, whether natural or man-made, and planting should be planned with these needs in mind. However, there is usually a latitude varying from a few inches to more than a foot with many plants, as you will also see in nature. It is also quite normal for plants to grow in different depths at various times of the year, as the water level drops in summer and rises in winter.

Establishing a new pond will give you a chance to provide all these different levels and thus extend the range of plants you can grow. For this reason, a sheet of butyl rubber which you can shape yourself will generally prove a more flexible pond liner, in every sense, than one pre-formed. Thick polythene can also be used but often breaks down after a few years. It is, however, important to lay any liner on a stone-free base, like soft sand or an old carpet, to prevent it being pierced by the weight of water over the years.

The different categories of water plants are as follows:

♦ Marginal plants

These plants, as the name implies, extend from the pond edge up to about 10–15cm (4–6in) deep. If planted in the water they need soil or compost in which to grow and initially must be anchored to the bottom with a piece of brick or tile, or the plants will float to the surface. Flints are ideal, but avoid ones with sharp edges.

Good native examples to grow are marsh marigold, which also does well in a marsh but which always looks better with the golden blooms reflected in water, water forget-me-not, water-plantain, grown mainly for the striking foliage as the spikes of white flowers are not very significant, and the fast-growing bogbean, with both attractive foliage and delicate, star-like white flowers. For a large pond, the flowering-rush is a most handsome plant but it grows up to 1.5m (5ft) tall and needs full sun for the rose-pink flowers to be seen at their best in late summer. On the shady side of a large pond, grow the magnificent royal fern which can reach 1.8m (6ft) tall so needs plenty of space to be seen at its lovely best.

◆ Submerged plants

These lie mainly under the water, either floating below the surface or rooted into the bottom of the pond, with any flowering shoots rising into the air. They are also known as oxygenators and play a very important part in the ecology of any pond by giving oxygen to the water and helping to prevent the excessive growth of algae.

The best native species are spiked water-milfoil, water-starwort and the rigid hornwort. They will obtain their root anchorage in the natural ooze at the bottom of the pond, but when planting weight them down with a stone to stop them floating to the surface. As the name implies, although widely grown and a good oxygenator, Canadian pondweed is not a native. Curled pondweed is an alternative native plant which is an equally good oxygenator and not so vigorous.

◆ Floating plants

These plants cover the surface with their leaves which lessens the amount of algae and are best typified by the water lily. For small ponds the best native water lily is the common yellow, which grows in water no more than 30cm (12in) deep. There is also a good native white species but this needs much deeper water to be successful. The more showy water lilies are mainly imports.

Other good floaters for small ponds are frogbit, with leaves rather like a water lily but with small white flowers, yellow-flowered greater bladderwort and the common water crowfoot, which has white flowers and is a good oxygenator but can be vigorous. All these need anchoring down initially, so that they can root into the bottom ooze which is also home to a range of wildlife. Water lilies need plenty of room for their roots and are best planted in a sunken net pot or basket, using soil-based compost, not peat, which will float.

◆ Deep-water plants

These are the plants which take over from marginals and float in the middle of the pond, in water up to several feet deep, with their flowers and foliage emerging through to the surface. They are generally only suitable for larger ponds as, in addition to needing deep water, they also take up a great deal of room on the surface. Two plants suitable for smaller ponds are the lilac-flowered water mint and arrowhead, which is named after the shape of the leaf and has white flowers.

◆ FLOWERING MEADOWS ◆

Another loss from the countryside over the past 50 years or so has been the enormous decline in the amount of permanent pasture and species-rich meadows. It has been calculated that possibly no more than 5 per cent of traditional lowland grass and 20 per cent of upland meadows and chalk downlands now remain.

It can come as quite a shock to travel in summer to an upland or alpine pasture in Austria or Switzerland and see the wealth of wild flowers still growing under an older form of grassland management. Intensive agriculture has caused their demise in our pastures.

However, the situation is now improving. Although the old forms of grassland management will themselves almost certainly never return, certainly on any large scale, the increase in amenity grassland, country parks and nature reserves is giving opportunity for the meadow flowers to be re-established. A number of local authorities, conservation-minded landowners and landscapers are now increasingly specifying suitable grass and wild flower mixes when sowing new grass areas and also ensuring that they are correctly managed. This will not restore the traditional permanent pastures and downlands, but at least it gives the wide range of meadow wild flowers a better chance of survival.

Gardeners can also play their part in helping preserve the flowers of the meadow, because they also control a very large area of grass. One possibility is to leave your lawn unweeded (page 12), when it will quite quickly be dominated by a number of vigorous plants like clover, daisy, dandelion, plantain, bird's-foot-trefoil and the speedwells. Some of these are, in fact, quite pretty and clover alone encourages the bees and helps the lawn stay green in a period of summer drought.

It is now possible to obtain mixtures of attractive low-growing, mainly perennial wild flowers intended to be sown with half the usual rate of lawn grass used to produce a colourful flower-rich lawn. These mixtures contain the more appropriate inhabitants of lawns (weeds!) together with suitable low-growing grassland flowers. All species should successfully withstand mowing if the lawn is cut at the height of 5–7cm/2–3in throughout the year except before and during the main flowering period (late May to early July) when it is left uncut.

Unless your soil is very thin and the sward very poor, a lawn is seldom the right place for encouraging the establishment of a rich collection of meadow wild flowers. The grasses it contains are too vigorous, the original seeding rate too high and, after possibly several years of applying lawn fertilizers, the soil will often be too fertile. Neither sowing nor planting a range of species into an established lawn is therefore usually very successful.

A flowering mini-meadow can, however, be established in most gardens big enough to support a lawn. The choice of site, soil preparation, sowing and management have already been dealt with (pages 12–13). Almost more important than any of these, however, is to choose the right mixture of flowers and grasses.

Specialist seedsmen now sell a range of mixtures suitable for different sites, soils and situations. Most contain about 80 per cent by weight of several fine leaved, relatively slow growing grasses mixed with about 20 per cent of 20 different species of wild flowers. Mixtures are available for open, partly shaded or wet conditions, sandy, heavy or loamy soils and also for those which are acid or alkaline. There are also late and early and flowering mixtures and others where the wild flowers are chosen to be attractive to butterflies.

The sort of grasses used include some common species like bents, fescues and meadow-grasses, but also some interesting wild species like sweet vernal-grass, yellow oat-grass, common quaking-grass, crested hair-grass and meadow barley. Left uncut until they have flowered, these will all give considerable interest to a flowering meadow. If making up your own meadow seed mixture, avoid at all costs vigorous grasses like the agricultural rye-grasses, cock's-foot, and timothy and try and eliminate the common weed grasses couch-grass and Yorkshire-fog before sowing. Most of them, even couch, have their place but will ruin the balance of a mini-meadow.

The wild flowers used in a meadow mixture are generally species which used to be found in grassland throughout the country. They are mostly relatively long-lived perennials plus a few annuals and biennials. Given the correct management, these will become established and continue to reproduce themselves either vegetatively or by seed, with a few annuals and biennials added. As most of the seed is collected by hand, it is not cheap, but sowing rates are lower than normally used for fine turf so the cost per square metre/yard is not excessive.

Wild thyme

A list of wild flowers for meadows in different situations is given on page 142–4, but among those most commonly used in mixtures are bird's-foot trefoil, black medick, cowslip, hoary and ribwort plantains, kidney vetch, lady's bedstraw, oxeye daisy, selfheal and yarrow. If these are allowed to flower and the mixture then cut and dried for hay, the mixture of flowers and grasses will give a blend of scent evocative of the old-fashioned countryside in summer.

Agriculturists declare that this blend of flowers and grasses in the old pastures gave no benefit to the meat or milk produced by the animals who grazed them. The modern, vigorous and often single species of grasses which are now grown and used in the production of hay and silage are no doubt nutritious and have helped in the greater production of quantity. Smelling the scented hay, however, there must be a suspicion of doubt about comparisons of quality.

◆ WILD FLOWERS FOR SMALL PLACES ◆

A mixed display of a reasonable number of our native plants can take a fair amount of space, which can be at a premium in some of today's gardens. However, even the smallest urban garden should be able to find space for a few selected wild flowers. Though the scale might be small, they will still bring their colour in from the countryside.

One approach is to find space for a rock garden and plant it with alpines. This can fit into any corner which is freely drained and gets plenty of sun. The term 'alpine' is a bit of a misnomer and often difficult to define. Originally it meant plants coming from alpine screes and meadows, then it covered plants from any hilly or mountain area and now the term seems used for almost any small or miniature plant. Having no alps, really there cannot be any native true alpines in Britain!

Many native mountain plants flower in the spring or early summer so that their seed can be set before the early onset of winter. By adding smaller, lowland species, you will extend the flowering season of the rock garden for a longer part of the year. This allows you to include a number of very colourful dwarf native wild flowers, which can be lost in a larger border.

One good place for a rock garden is alongside a garden pond. In this way you can use the soil excavated from the pond as the foundation and the contrast between a raised rock garden and the lower pond can be most pleasing. Amphibians from the pond like newts and toads will also enjoy climbing on to the rocks to sun themselves.

A garden on a sunny slope provides a good site for a rock garden. Here you can place one or two large rocks so that they jut out of the slope to look like a natural outcrop, using smaller stones to form pockets and crevices in which to grow the plants. On a level site it is generally best to make the rock garden in the shape of a mound, which helps the drainage and gives you a bigger planting area than if you plant on the flat.

When building a rock garden, the first rule is to construct it using the same type of rock or stone throughout. If possible, try and obtain the local stone of the area. Should you live in a rockless area, weathered limestone is probably the best to buy but sandstone is also quite suitable and will often be considerably cheaper.

Whatever type of stones you use, try to arrange them with the 'grain' of each running in the same direction so that they look as natural as possible. A common mistake is to use too many stones; remember that you are aiming to give a natural looking home to a blend of plants, not trying to reproduce a rocky mountainside. At all costs, avoid using for your rock garden pieces of broken concrete paving stone from the council tip or the collection of rocks of all sorts you have brought back in the car boot from trips around the country – they seldom mix happily together.

Mountain and hill plants mostly come from areas of high rainfall but very free drainage. Nearly all will grow well in a good garden soil but they will not tolerate too much water around the roots, especially in winter. This is also true of many small lowland plants, many of which will survive hard frosts and cold winds quite happily provided they are not also asked to tolerate wet feet.

Unless your garden soil is a fibrous, open loam, and few are, you will give all the plants a better start by planting them in pockets of prepared compost. This can be made on the spot by adding peat and a sharp grit to your own soil or buying in a proper John Innes-type compost. Peat-based composts are less suitable unless they contain added grit. Granite or limestone chippings added as a surface dressing after planting will add an authentic look to your rock garden and also help retain moisture. They can be bought from any good garden shop or centre.

Good native mountain plants suitable for the rock garden include mountain avens, a lovely plant with white flowers and golden centres and evergreen leaves, the golden common rock-rose, the pink wild thyme, which will creep over stones and nearby paths and be covered in bees, the long-flowering and trailing yellow tormentil, alpine lady's mantle, similar in colour and form to the larger lowland species and, if you have an acid soil, the native species of heather. To these can be added a wide range of other dwarf and small plants like thrift, also very good for the edge of ponds, the blue harebell and its relative the clustered bellflower. Pasqueflower, now very rare in the wild, the bright red bloody crane's-bill and sea campion which is smaller than others in the same family and carries large, double white flowers over attractive waxy foliage are also suitable.

A dwarf garden wall will also make another useful site for wild flowers, even if it only forms the boundary for the front garden. Dry-stone walls with plenty of natural crevices are the best but old brick walls with the odd brick missing can also be made to look very attractive. New brick walls can be more difficult; one solution is to build a double wall with plants growing in the gap between.

In addition to many from the rock garden, walls can also be used for some colourful trailing plants like ivy-leaved toadflax, stonecrop and yellow corydalis, which is actually not a true native but is now a widespread introduction. All these can be planted either at the bottom of a wall to grow up, or on top to grow down.

Another use for walls is to restrict plants which, although colourful, can be rather too vigorous or invasive in an open border. In this category come herb-robert, a pretty annual relative of the crane's-bill which will self-seed profusely if allowed, the true yellow-flowering wallflower, again not an original native but now widely distributed, and several native species of stonecrop which, if left unchecked, can soon take over a rock garden. A taller, unsightly wall can be used to support several wild climbers like honeysuckle, traveller's-joy and the wild hop and so give an added vertical dimension to a garden.

An additional way to add an extra dimension to a small garden space is to plant wild flowers in containers such as patio tubs, window boxes, large pots and hanging baskets. Many rock garden and other small plants grow very well in these containers, either on their own or in combination with cultivated plants.

One plant worthy of especial mention is wild pansy, or heart's-ease, which is equally as worth growing in a basket or tub as its popular cultivated cousin. A good way to grow it is to sow the seed in July, prick the seedlings out in small pots or boxes and plant up the containers in September. Some flowers will appear during the first autumn but flowering starts again in early spring and provided the plants are kept dead-headed and watered, will last through until at least late summer.

• FINAL THOUGHTS •

This chapter has demonstrated a number of ways that wild flowers can be grown and the wide variety of habitats which can be chosen or adapted. There are several others which could be added: gardens by the sea making use of salt tolerant and sea-marsh plants or plants found growing in sand dunes, gardens for converted sand or chalk pits, sandy heaths, clearings in woodland – even disused railway have been used to make a home for wild flowers.

As with all gardening, you can observe what grows well in the natural surroundings, study the characteristics of the plants you want to grow, give the ideal conditions but in the end much will come back to trial and error. If you are prepared to experiment with wild flowers, even if the situation looks unpromising, they are tolerant and adaptable enough to often surprise you with the results.

Sunny mixed borders show: common poppy, perennial flax and red campion (*left*); cowslip, meadow saxifrage and purple wild pansy (*above right*); and wild clary, oxeye daisy, thrift, common rock-rose, bloody crane's-bill (*below right*).

TRADITIONAL USES FOR WILD FLOWERS

S ome gardeners will be content to plant a range of wild flowers into their gardens and just admire them for their form and colour. Others might like to consider more deeply the history of our native plants, how traditionally they were used in the past, what they can still be used for today, plus the extra dimension this can bring to a garden.

Although we owe a large debt of gratitude to the Victorians for the great changes they brought to our gardens in their search for the novel and exotic, some things also were lost. A knowledge of the traditional uses of many native plants was one of them and it has taken until the latter part of the present century to help restore our sense of values. As well as being pleasant to look at, indigenous plants still have many uses.

• FLOWER ARRANGING •

In the village flower shows of one's youth, one of the most interesting classes for children used to be the collection of wild flowers. Such collections could often contain up to 30–40 different species and although usually not strictly flower arrangements, they showed what a range of colour and forms could be picked from the countryside.

Nowadays few districts could produce such collections from the wild. With the reduced numbers of flowers, it would also be rather irresponsible to encourage children to pick them. With the current revival of village flower shows, horticultural societies might, however, consider including a class in the schedule for a collection of garden-grown wild flowers. This would be an eye-opener for those who at the moment might regard them as 'just a lot of weeds'.

Displays by flower clubs, on the other hand, show that flower arrangers now often include indigenous material like grasses, ferns and bark to give some interesting effects. Here again, native flowers could be more widely used instead of the exotics from overseas which are generally preferred. In addition, how often do we see the type of flower festival once encountered in a tiny church in the heart of Suffolk, where only cottage garden and native-type flowers were used in very simple arrangements? A flower festival based entirely on cultivated wild flowers, late-summer fruits and berries could be equally impressive.

Species which enjoy a slightly shaded position include red campion (*above*), bluebell (*below left*) which is best planted around shrubs and trees and tufted vetch the colourful climber (*below right*).

Of course, just as with normal border flowers, not every wild flower is suitable for cutting. The evening-primroses, for example, are too short-lived whilst the common comfrey, although a very decorative plant, is one which will not take up water once it is cut. By far the majority, however, cut very well, though care is needed to keep them at their best. Always try and gather the flowers either early in the morning or in the evening, when they can be stood in a bucket of deep water overnight before being arranged the following day. Flowers with thick, solid stems need to be bruised or split to encourage them to take up water. This is not needed for hollow stemmed plants, but they can benefit from the stems being inverted and filled with water before being arranged in bowls or vases. The common poppy will wilt rapidly unless the bottoms of the sappy stems are scorched or plunged in boiling water to stop them bleeding.

Dissolving a flower preservative in the water has been shown to lengthen the life of most flowers by discouraging the production of bacteria and providing a food supply. Even more important, however, is to always use and top up with clean, fresh water and to wash all containers between uses to prevent the growth of algae. Bulbous flowers such as bluebells and the wild daffodil also produce a slime which encourages bacteria, so their water needs changing fairly often.

Amongst the best species of wild flowers for large displays are a number of common countryside favourites which last well in water. These include yarrow, oxeye daisy, yellow corn marigold, blue annual cornflower, both white and red campions, the related pink ragged-robin and several of the mallows. For table centres and posies a good supply of snowdrops, violets, primroses, cowslips and ground-ivy will prove invaluable in spring, with thrift, daisy, cuckoo flower or lady's bedstraw and the leaves and flowers of bugle used later in the summer. A large vase of foxgloves makes a striking display in a fireplace or in a corner of a hall and honeysuckle will fill the house with fragrance in summer, though it goes over rather quickly and the dropped flowers can make rather a mess.

◆ PRESERVING AND PRESSING ◆
WILD FLOWERS

To continue the pleasure they give when fresh, the flowers, leaves and seedheads of almost any plant can be dried and preserved and this is equally true of wild flowers. Like normal garden plants, some are worth preserving more than others and it is usually best to concentrate on flowers which retain either a very distinctive colour or perfume. Leaves of ferns, grasses, ivy and trees like oak and beech also preserve well and can be invaluable for adding to a mixed dried flower arrangement.

It is very important to harvest all plant material at the right time for preserving. If the often delicate colour is to be maintained, plants like lady's mantle, for example, need picking in full flower and well before they start to fade. Seedheads should be picked when mature but before the seed is distributed, unless you want to display the open pod. Grasses also need picking in full flower and before the pollen is formed; green leaves can be taken at any time after they are fully expanded, unless you aim to preserve their autumn colours.

There are several methods of flower and plant preservation. Air drying is undoubtedly the simplest method and the most common. All you need is a room which is kept dry and airy and not too warm, but with a minimum temperature of 10°C (50°F). This can be a spare bedroom or attic, or in summer even the roof or a garage or garden shed. High humidity must be avoided and a fan can be useful to circulate air in muggy weather.

Depending on their form and shape, flowers, grasses and leaves can be dried either laid flat, or hung in bunches, which is especially suitable for plants with decorative seedheads such as docks, cow parsley, poppy and teasel. They can also be dried standing in a bucket or basket, but with flower sprays this can lead to bending of the tips. Really large seedheads can be supported singly on a rack made of small-mesh wire netting.

Many leaves are best preserved with glycerine, which keeps them supple and means they retain their shape when dried. The main disadvantage of glycerine-treated material is that it sometimes loses its colour and turns brown. For this reason it is usually better for preserving leaves and stems than flowers.

This technique involves mixing 60 per cent hot water and 40 per cent glycerine, allowing this to cool and then standing the stems 7–10cm (3–4in) deep in it. Hard wood stems must be cut or bruised to make sure the solution is absorbed. Keep the container in the cool and dark whilst the glycerine is taken in by the leaves and stems and the water content gradually evaporates. Depending on the plant material, this will take up to about 10 days and is complete once all the solution is absorbed. Large individual leaves or shoots of softer plants can be preserved individually in glycerine. In this case, use a 50/50 mixture with hot water and immerse the leaves or shoots totally, remove once they have changed colour, wash off the glycerine with warm water and detergent and lay on newspaper to dry.

Dessication is a third way of preserving flowers by extracting their water content but maintaining almost the original colour. Drying agents used to dessicate are silica gel, borax and soap powder.

Silica gel dries out plant material very quickly and can be used repeatedly for several batches. It can be bought either as white crystals or with a built-in colour indicator which turns pink when moist and blue when dry. To use it you will need a tin or jar which can be air-sealed. Place a layer of dry crystals 1.2cm (½in) thick into this container and lay the heads of flowers, which can be individually wired, on top of them. Add more crystals until the flowers are completely covered, then close the container and seal it with sellotape. Make sure that the individual shapes of the flowers are not crushed or distorted.

Once the moisture indicator shows that moisture has been removed from the flowers, they can be removed from the crystals. This should only take a few days; to leave them any longer can turn the flowers brittle. The crystals can be dried in an oven for re-use, but be careful to store them in an air-tight container.

Borax powder can also be used in a similar way but drying will take at least twice as long as with silica gel. The mixture can again be re-dried for further use. Another cheap and readily available material which can be used for dessication is pure soap powder – not the 'biological' types which contain a detergent and sometimes cause loss of colour. This dries flowers very well but the powder must be quite dry and free-flowing

◆ FLOWER PRESSING ◆

Here we go back to the reign of Victoria, when the ability to press flowers was a required accomplishment of every well-born lady. It was also often coupled with a great surge of interest in botany and the study of plants in general.

Pressing is a very easy way of drying flowers and can often retain their colour in almost perfect natural condition. Quite simple methods can be used for pressing, such as placing flowers under heavy books or leaves and ferns between sheets of newspaper under the living-room carpet, but the best results will come from a simple type of flower press. These can now be bought from many craft shops, or you can make one quite easily.

For this you will need two square sheets of thick plywood to form the top and base, four long, threaded bolts and wing nuts to connect them and seven or eight alternate layers of newspaper and cardboard to go in between. The cardboard must be thick enough to prevent the shape of one layer of flowers being impressed on the next below or above, for which corrugated card is ideal. Blotting paper is better than newspaper if you have some available.

All plant material used for pressing must be cut dry and placed in the press soon after cutting, ensuring that it forms only a single layer and none of it overlaps. Air and temperature conditions should be similar to air drying. The press need not be filled completely at one time, but if adding layers, make sure the flowers and leaves already in it are not disturbed.

The drying process will take several weeks, depending on the size and thickness of the individual leaves and flowers. If you intend eventually to dissect the flowers and use individual petals, this is best done before pressing. Most of the small wild flowers, many grasses, ferns and leaves can all be pressed successfully, though the most pleasing results will come from those which have either outstanding colours or shapes.

Once thoroughly dried, pressed flowers can be used to make very colourful pictures which, if covered with glass and kept out of the direct sun, will keep their colour for many years. You could also use them to make a wild flower collection book and for greetings cards, covering the flowers with either clear Fablon or similar types of film to protect them. Pressed flowers can also look most attractive when mounted on cards placed under glass or Perspex door plates. Here, arrangements of individual petals of, for example, the rose-pink rosebay willowherb are often more effective than complete flowers.

◆ THE FRAGRANCE OF WILD FLOWERS ◆

In medieval times, a number of native wild flowers were used for their fragrance. Lacking our standards of hygiene and plumbing, nosegays were often carried by the more delicate when they were forced to mingle with the malodorous masses. This custom is still carried on today with a nosegay carried by the Queen at her annual distribution of the Maundy pence.

Posies and nosegays were also carried by maidens to attract lovers by their perfume, frequently using the clove pink, brought to this country by the Normans and an ancestor of the modern border carnation, wild wallflower which they knew as gilly flower and milkwort, a rather insignificant plant but with flowers varying from white to blue and purple and a delicate fragrance. Similar scented flowers were also used in the church, both to decorate shrines and as garlands for the priests.

In the days when beaten earth formed the floor of even churches and manor houses, wild flowers were strewn with the rushes which formed the normal floor covering to help hide the musty odours caused by damp and a lack of ventilation. Meadowsweet was one flower which Queen Elizabeth liked strewn in the royal apartments, and she also had a member of the household whose sole task was to provide fresh flowers and herbs to cover the floors in all seasons.

In an earlier century, Thomas à Beckett is recorded as ordering May blossom to be spread on the floors in spring and sweet-scented rushes in summer. Spreading scented wild flowers was still being carried out in the reign of George IV, with an official herb strewer, assisted by six young ladies, appointed by him for his coronation. In the same century, aromatic herbs were strewn in the dock of the central criminal court at the Old Bailey to guard against jail fever.

Times change but even nowadays there are several domestic uses for some of our scented wild flowers. Hanging up bunches of tansy, pennyroyal or water mint will help to deter house flies and is cheaper than buying cans of aerosol. Dried sweet woodruff will help deter moths from clothes and gives linen a smell of new-mown hay. The wild hop has been re-discovered as a filling for pillows to help the insomniac and these are now sold commercially.

Our fragrant wild flowers can also be used as ingredients for the increasingly popular pot-pourri. This term, meaning literally 'rotten pot', was applied originally to a mixture of rose petals and salt taken into a sick room. Nowadays there are a number of different recipes, most of which are based on mixtures of strongly-scented dried flower petals and leaves, combined with a strong-smelling essence or oil. Wild flowers which can be added to these mixtures include violet, lily-of-the-valley, honeysuckle, pinks, sweet woodruff and wild mignonette.

◆ MEDICINAL USES ◆

Every country has its folk-tradition of using native plants for medicine and Britain is no exception. Even though some cures came perilously near to witchcraft, since time began all sorts of lotions and potions have been made from local plants, often growing in abundance. Even the Garden of Eden, one supposes, contained other useful plants apart from an apple tree.

It seems rather ironic to find the vast, affluent pharmaceutical industry using its resources to identify and synthesise modern drugs often based on past herbal remedies. A number of well-established herbal remedies are themselves coming back into fashion, though sometimes given a fancier and more up-to-date name. With these old-fashioned remedies it can come as a surprise to find that granny, in fact, quite often did know best.

This is not to decry modern medicine in any way, nor to claim for the old herbal remedies more than they ever achieved. We should be very thankful for the great advance made by science in the present century and the greater health of the population that this has brought. Without our modern knowledge, the lack of cure for really serious diseases was one of the reasons that life for many of our ancestors has been fairly accurately described as nasty, brutal and short. Modern conditions may have encouraged some stress-related diseases, but many of us are now living longer and statistics show that the health of the nation has never been in better general shape.

Nevertheless, as part of our cultural tradition if nothing else, it is interesting to know about some of these old country remedies. A number come from using quite common plants and a collection of species which had medicinal uses can make an interesting addition to a wild flower garden. Whether you then use any of them for their original medicinal purpose is then entirely up to you. Be careful, however, in untutored hands some plants can be quite dangerous and it would be safest to stick to simple remedies like those for tonic drinks and cough linctus. For any more serious conditions you should consult your doctor or a qualified herbal practitioner. A selection of popular treatments is given below.

◆ Colds, coughs and sneezes

An infusion of fresh or dried elderflowers mixed with yarrow and peppermint can be taken at the first sign of a cold and with honey added will give considerable relief to a sore throat. A hot drink made from elderberries, with or without blackcurrant juice and also sweetened with honey, will sooth a sore throat and coughs. Chamomile can be used either as a gargle or by inhalation, common calamint can be made into a soothing syrup, while horehound, colt's-foot and comfrey can all be drunk as teas to ease catarrh. One of the oldest known remedies for a cough is to take a tisane, or infusion, of a dried mixture of coltsfoot leaves, ground ivy leaves and marsh-mallow root.

◆ Soothing a fever or a headache

Meadowsweet has many of the properties of aspirin, itself derived originally from the bark of a willow, taken as an infusion between meals. Lungwort, alkanet, viper's-bugloss, sorrel and purslane can all be used in a similar way. Feverfew was once widely used against fevers and as aid to digestion and there is growing medical evidence to show that two or three leaves eaten each day will benefit a majority of migraine sufferers.

◆ Invigorating tonics

Herbal tonics were once especially useful during winter months, when diet was more limited and there was a shortage of fresh fruit and vegetables. Many of these have since been shown to be rich in either vitamins or natural essential minerals. Infusions can be made from the leaves of the nettle, dandelion, blackberry, chickweed, good-King-Henry, cleavers or goosegrass, plantain and several others, either on their own or as a mixture. Some of them can also be chopped and added to a salad. Even bindweed was regarded as a particularly useful cleanser of the blood, either eaten raw or with the stems made into a tea, whilst the horsetail family is rich in many vitamins and minerals.

◆ Aids to the digestion

Some of these are also tonics used in spring to help stimulate a sluggish appetite after a limited winter diet. They were often very bitter to the taste, so were not used in large quantities, and probably did a similar job to the peppers and spices used in hotter climates. They included powdered root of the native field gentian, the leaves and roots of dandelion and chicory and infusions of the root of bogbean and the leaves of horehound, mugwort and wood sage. Mild bowel stimulants include dandelion root and elder leaf while yarrow was used to clear the skin and cleavers to encourage kidney activity. Binding plants include common agrimony, common bistort, meadowsweet, plantain and wood avens.

◆ First aid

Cuts and bruises can be washed with either a solution, infusion or poultice made from a number of plants including elder leaves, agrimony, common bistort, chamomile, colt's-foot, common comfrey, cleavers, horsetail, lady's-mantle, plantain, St John's-wort and yarrow. For aches and pains add an infusion of ground elder leaves and roots to the bath, or drink a tisane made from dandelion or nettle. Sprains can be treated with a compress of agrimony, common comfrey, common mallow, St John's-wort or vervain, insect bites rubbed with leaves of docks, common comfrey, marsh mallow or the mints, corns and warts with the juice of the greater celandine. Chilblains can be treated by drinking a daily dose in cold weather of a tisane made from rose hips or horsetail, to stimulate the circulation.

This is just a selection of the remedies available from wild flowers grown in your garden; a good herbalist will tell you of many more.

◆ THE FRUITS OF THE EARTH ◆

A wide range of British plants have always provided useful edible pickings for those prepared to gather them. Leaves, fruits, berries, stems and even flowers from the wild have all been used by country dwellers in the past to supplement the produce from their gardens. There is also a strong body of opinion which still says that the field mushroom, when it can be found, is tastier than its cultured cousin, brambles have a sweeter flavour than cultivated blackberries, the wild crab makes the best apple jelly and bullace is better in a fruit pie than any modern plum.

Over 150 species of our native wild flowers and plants are edible in one way or another. A number of them can be quite hard to find, however, and you might not be allowed access to where others are growing. Although some are still quite common, other rarer species should either not now be picked at all or only taken very sparingly. It is against the law, of course, to harvest any part of a protected plant. As with medicinal plants, the answer might well be to grow some of the most useful in your garden, either as a separate culinary bed, possibly in with other herbs, or in a mixed flowering border. Grown in this way you can be sure that they have not been contaminated in any way by herbicides, pesticides or even inorganic fertilizers.

A word of caution is needed about the culinary use of wild plants. The flavour is frequently much stronger than cultivated sorts and when trying a new one for the first time, it is always best to err on the side of moderation. The taste and texture of many leaves can also change as they get older, so always try and pick them when they are young and at their most succulent. Some roots can coarsen and become fibrous as they thicken, so, here again, choose the youngest available.

◆ Edible leaves and stems

There are leaves from a number of plants that can be eaten raw, usually as an ingredient of a mixed salad. Some grow quite early and others late in the year, so can help extend the salad season. Watercress has always been one of the most highly regarded, though most of what we buy today is grown commercially. The wild form is identical, but should only be gathered from fast-running and unpolluted water and never from near where sheep are grazing as it harbours one of the parasites. Other edible members of the same family growing on dry land are field penny-cress, hairy bitter-cress and the related lady's-smock, and both white and garlic mustard, also known as Jack-by-the-hedge.

Dandelion leaves have long been known as a nutritious fresh vegetable but have never been so popular here as in some other countries, possibly because they can be rather bitter. Always pick the youngest leaves and make them sweeter by blanching (excluding the light from) plants growing in the garden by covering with either peat or soil. Foliage of other members of the same family which can be eaten includes nipplewort, cat's-ear, rough hawkbit, goat's-beard and wall lettuce.

Leaves which can be chopped and sprinkled over a salad include salad burnet, now being more widely grown as a garden herb, sorrel, wild strawberry and golden saxifrage, which adds an attractive colour.

Nettles are one of the most widely available leaves. It can be cooked as a replacement for spinach, made into soup or used for nettle beers and tea. There is even a recipe for nettle haggis. Both the perennial common or stinging nettle and the annual or small nettle are suitable but cut them regularly to maintain a supply of young, succulent shoots.

Other useful leaves for cooking include common comfrey, fat-hen and the related good-King-Henry, now grown increasingly as a herb, common orache and chickweed. Found on virtually every allotment and vegetable patch, the latter grows for long periods of the year and can make a useful vegetable supplement when lightly simmered in a mixture with chopped chives or spring onions. Cleavers or goosegrass is another common weed of both cultivated and waste ground which can be picked and cooked like spinach in the winter, when the young shoots are still fresh. In hard times the seeds are said to have been roasted as an alternative for coffee.

The large-leaved and stately alexanders were once grown in kitchen gardens but have since become naturalised wild plants. The most widely used part is the leaf stem, 15cm/6in lengths of which are cut off near the base, cooked for about 10 minutes and can be eaten like asparagus with butter. The leaves and flower buds have also been added to salads and a soup made from the roots. Other plant stems which have been used include burdock, the marsh and rock samphires and several thistles.

◆ Edible roots

Although not strictly a native, horse-radish is now widely naturalised in waste places such as railway embankments and large quantities are also cultivated for commercial use. Unlike many plants, the thickest roots are the best and need all the outside brown skin removed before grating.

Also very plentiful in the countryside are the wild ancestors of many of our common root vegetables, including wild carrot, wild parsnip, wild turnip and wild radish. They might be worth tasting for the experience but really cannot compare with their better bred descendants. Dandelion root can be dried and ground as a caffeine-free alternative to coffee, but is an acquired taste.

One old custom which might be revived is digging for pignut. The dark brown 'nuts' of this pretty, white, wayside flower are really swollen roots or small tubers growing $2\frac{1}{2}$–5cm/1–2in below the surface, from which they should be dug up and not pulled by the stem – which kills the plant and usually loses the nut. Eaten by the wayside as a child they only had a quick wipe with a handkerchief, but brought indoors they can be washed and scraped before adding them to a salad.

◆ Flowers

A widespread culinary use for wild flowers has always been for making home-made wine, and very good they can be too. Elderflower is a favourite and the best may fairly be compared with a good German Mosel. Elderflowers also give an added flavour to gooseberry jam, placed in a muslin bag for a first boiling and removed before adding the sugar. Cowslips make another popular country wine but because a gallon of flowers are needed to make a gallon of wine, gathering them may have helped hasten the disappearance of this flower in some areas. Other recipes for native flower wines include broom, clover, dandelion and hawthorn or May blossom. You can also use either fresh or dried wild hop flowers for brewing beer, and a liqueur can be made from hawthorn flowers steeped in brandy.

Elderflower champagne is a non-alcoholic cooling summer drink which is very quick and easy to make. There are also a number of teas which can be made from dried wild flowers including those of the lime, heather and chamomile, either on their own or mixed with other flowers and leaves. Such 'herbal teas' have once again become fashionable and a number are now commercially available.

A final culinary use for flowers is to use them to add flavour and colour to salads, scattering a few edible flowers or petals of plants like violets, dog-rose, broom, daisy and primrose as a final dressing.

◆ Fruits

Most of the fruits and nuts native to this country grow best wild in hedgerows and woodlands and few are really suitable as garden plants. A surprisingly large variety is still there to be picked in late-summer and autumn, though sometimes there can be problems from landowners not allowing access. Fruits of the crab apple, elder, bramble sloe, rowan or mountain ash and bilberry can be used for jellies, hips from the dog-rose make a syrup high in vitamin C, good country wines are made from crab, elderberry and bramble, whilst very potent sloe gin is only recommended in moderation – and never when driving!

One fruiting plant which should be planted in any garden collection of native flowers is the wild strawberry. Although the fruits are much smaller than cultivated varieties, the tedium of picking them is rewarded by their sweeter flavour. You may well only grow enough to eat fresh with cream, sugar should not be needed, but they also make a very sweet and dark jam and are quite superb as a filling for tarts.

◆ Flavourings

A number of the popular aromatic herbs used for flavouring are not native but come from the Mediterranean region, where their scent can be almost over-powering in the southern sunshine. Our wild herbs generally are not so pungent but their delicate flavour can be equally useful in cooking. A number can be used both fresh during the growing season and dried for the winter. Air-drying normally is sufficient (page 51).

Sometimes these uses are described by their names. Meadowsweet, for example, is a corruption derived from the use of the leaves to give an aroma to mead and other wine and not because it grew in a meadow. Woodruff was usually given the prefix 'sweet' and used for a similar purpose. Other plants in this group are sweet cicely, which in this case refers to the sweetness it adds to stewed fruits, and sweet gale, more properly called bog-myrtle and used to flavour beer before the discovery of hops. The aromatic leaves of fennel are used to flavour eggs or fish, angelica to add to rhubarb, wild marjoram for meat and wild thyme as a highly scented alternative to the cultivated type for stuffings. If you are fond of garlic, try the native species called ramsons or wood-garlic.

WILDLIFE GARDENS

· GARDENS TO ATTRACT WILDLIFE ·

It would be nonsense to suggest that only wild flowers and native trees and shrubs can attract wildlife into a garden. By their nature, insects such as butterflies and bees know no boundaries and birds and animals have only survived in the cut and thrust of the wild by learning very quickly to become adaptable. Just as they adapted to the past creation of hedges and woodland, so they will move to wherever there appears to be a living.

However, as natural habitats become fewer, gardens can provide sanctuary for a wide range of wildlife species. Although present-day countryside planting schemes of broad-leaved trees, together with the encouragement and conservation of indigenous plants, should help eventually to restore a natural balance, gardens will always remain an alternative haven. They can offer in particular a mixture of native and more exotic plants which wildlife will find appealing.

'Use' is the key, wildlife is attracted to areas when it can firstly, feed and survive and secondly, reproduce. Especially attractive to butterflies are cultivated shrubs like buddleia, hebe, syringa and senecio; the herbaceous plants Michaelmas daisy; catmint, ice plant; the red valerian, berberis, honeysuckle, cotoneaster, pyracantha; the viburnums and many border plants for bees; and a number of conifers for ladybirds. Birds, both locals like the blackbird and migrants such as waxwing, will feed avidly on berries and fruits of flowering crab, chaenomeles, skimmia, mountain ash, whitebeam, symphoricarpus and a host of others.

So a designer-garden for wildlife should ideally contain a wide range of plant species and habitats. There is no reason why it has to be a jungle, but although most of the garden can still be kept tidy, there should be some quiet and undisturbed corners. It will also help if you can leave small areas of complete wilderness, like nettles and other undergrowth left growing round the back of a shed or garage for butterflies, dead wood left to rot as a home for beetles, brambles trailing over a wall or tree to give a nesting site for birds and an untrimmed hedge bottom to provide a home for small mammals like field mice.

Just to grow a mixture of wild and cultivated plants to give food and shelter is probably, however, the best help you can give to wildlife. Having grown the plants and established the habitats do not expect a wide range of wildlife to appear immediately. It can take time, especially if you live in the middle of a new housing development, or in a country cottage surrounded by many acres of farmland with few hedge 'pathways' to lead the wildlife to you. Eventually the butterflies, insects, birds and others will come and appreciate your wildlife garden; like humans, they know a good thing when they find it.

Which brings us to the delicate subject of cats. Some of us will know cat-lovers who swear their cats never eat songbirds, but the fact has to be faced that they are predators of wildlife and as a recent study of urban gardens has shown, very efficient ones indeed. Even if you do not keep a cat yourself, being no respecter of boundaries, unless you are very isolated they will soon come in from the neighbourhood. So if you are surrounded by cats, your own or others, you might not be so lucky with the birds and the animals but have to concentrate more on attracting the butterflies and bees.

◆ PLANTS FOR BUTTERFLIES AND MOTHS ◆

A well-established garden with plenty of sources of nectar should be full of a range of butterflies from spring until autumn. Do not, however, expect a large number to arrive immediately. Populations will need to build up in a previously flower-starved area, some species will not be native to your locality and others only visit us as migrants from Europe, so they might not get here in a bad summer.

Many butterflies are highly adaptable and will feed on a wide range of flowers and other sweet sources, like the honeydew secreted by some greenflies and even fallen, rotted apples. Providing breeding sites can be slightly more difficult. Nettles, for example, are favoured by several species but as butterflies can be fickle, they need to be on a sunny site and in the right young condition for when the eggs are laid. To feel really at home, butterflies also favour a garden surrounded by hedges, both to give summer shelter and as a hibernation site for some adults and pupae over winter.

Flowers favoured by butterflies may not always be those most attractive to the human eye. Luckily some are and they include the common and greater knapweed, field and devil's-bit scabious, ragged-robin and soapwort. Creeping thistle is not attractive to most gardeners but unfortunately is a particularly good supplier of nectar to butterflies, whilst the rather sombre flowers, buds and berries of the native ivy are much better for them than the often more colourful cultivated varieties and species. Common fleabane is also not an especially useful plant in the garden, except in a very wet spot, but is a valuable supplier of food.

Nettles are used for breeding by the small tortoishell, peacock, comma and red admiral, whilst the comma also favours the wild hop and elder. Painted lady, on the other hand, prefers thistles and the holly blue both holly and ivy. The orange tip, the females of which must not be confused with the more common cabbage white, breeds on lady's-smock and both hedge and garlic mustard. Although the caterpillars eat some leaves, some damage seems worth enduring for the sake of seeing the early-flying adults.

One good reason to establish a mini-meadow in your garden is that it helps encourage meadowland butterflies like meadow brown, the gatekeeper and the small blue. All these are attracted by a sward of fairly long grass containing a mixture of flowering plants, on which they will both feed and lay their eggs. Some will pupate on long grass over winter, couch grass being an especial favourite, so this is a good reason not to make your final autumn grass cut too short. Shorter grass is also attractive to the common blue and in some areas the dingy skipper, but it must also contain a few low-growing wild flowers like the clovers, thyme and common bird's-foot-trefoil if they are to both feed and breed.

Several moths are also worth a mention, as they can be encouraged by growing nectar-supplying plants. Although the large, voracious caterpillars of the mullein moth, for example, devour the equally large, woolly leaves of the great mullein, there are plenty of leaves to go at and a bit of damage seems worth enduring to keep this species alive.

The well-known 'woolly bear' caterpillar of the tiger moth, on the other hand, actually acts as a gardener's friend. It eats a number of common weeds like groundsel, chickweed, dock and dandelion but it will need a regular food supply to become established – a good reason for not being too hasty with the hoe. As night-flyers, the parent moths will normally only be seen at night when attracted by lamps or a lighted window. An exception is the migrant humming-bird hawk moth, which is a fairly common visitor to flowers by day.

◆ PLANTS FOR BEES AND OTHER INSECTS ◆

Whilst enjoying the beauty of butterflies is something of a pleasant luxury, bees and other beneficial insects are an important working part of many gardens. Although wind and other mechanisms also play their part, it is this group of pollinators which are responsible for setting vegetables like runner beans and giving larger and better formed crops of fruit. Thus, by making your garden more attractive to them, many crops in the vegetable and fruit sections will benefit and you will also help the ecological balance. On a summer's day there is also considerable satisfaction to be had from listening to the hum of the bees and watching the play of other insects around your flowers.

Since bee keeping has declined, due to a combination of factors such as economics, disease, harder winters and poorer summers and the damage done to colonies by agricultural spraying, so the wild bee has become more important. This is especially true in the spring, when it can be too cold for the hive bees to work and the bumble and other wild bees are essential to ensure early fruit pollination. If you look at an April-flowering gooseberry bush, for example, you will find that it is invariably the bumble and not the hive bee which is busily at work.

A mixture of both cultivated and wild flowers is needed to ensure a good supply of pollen and nectar needed by both the wild and honey bees. As with butterflies, this means planning your garden to give continuity of flowers right through the year, from the snowdrops and other early bulbs through to late flowerers like the ice plant in the autumn. Even the winter-flowering shrubs can be be visited by bees on a pleasant day in January.

Some wild flowers have quite elaborate flowering mechanisms which only allow one specific type of insect to pollinate them. The white dead-nettle, for example, is formed so that only the long tongue of a bumble bee can reach the nectar. This ensures that it also comes into contact with pollen carried on the stamens, which the bee then carries on its back to cross-fertilise the next plant it visits. A number of wild plants, like the foxglove and mallow for example, have markings on them called honey guides which lead the bee into the flowers. In some species this is only visible under ultra-violet light.

Wild flowers especially attractive to bumble bees are the wood anemone, the knapweeds, thistles, traveller's-joy, common hawkweed, field scabious and field poppy. These will also be attractive to hive bees but others which will give them a good supply of both pollen and nectar include the clustered bellflower, tansy, viper's-bugloss, common toad-flax, bird's-foot-trefoil and bluebell.

Another major group of pollinating insects are the hover-flies, sometimes mistaken for a type of wasp. These take nectar from flowers in large numbers, especially in a warm and sunny autumn. Earlier in the year they are attracted to members of the carrot family like hogweed and cow parsley. Hover-flies are also an important predator of greenfly, which they consume in large numbers.

Pre-eminent as a garden predator of greenfly is, of course, the ladybird. It appears to have no major function as a pollinator and no preference for individual flowers. It would be an even better predator if so many were not lost during winter hibernation, so that the population built up in early summer rather than later. This can be helped by not disturbing ladybirds during hibernation, but if any emerge in the warmth indoors, supply a little moisture on a leaf so that they do not dehydrate and put them back in the cool of a shed or outhouse.

With ladybirds, bees of all kinds, hover-flies, harmless beetles and other insects it is also most important to be careful with spraying any pesticides. If you must use any sort of chemical, keep sprays to the minimum and away from any beneficial insects that are present, never spray open flowers, do not spray in windy weather and only spray early in the morning or late in the evening when flying insects are likely to be less active.

◆ BIRD LIFE ◆

Somewhat like cats, birds in a garden can be a difficult subject. There is no doubt that some can cause a great deal of damage, both to crops of fruit and the destruction of the buds and flowers of primrose, daphne and forsythia – to name but a few. At the same time, many other birds are good controllers of pests like caterpillars, slugs, snails and wireworm. There are also the benefits of birdsong, the extra colour and interest birds bring to a garden plus the opportunity to provide a haven for species whose future may be in the balance.

The answer, surely, is to welcome birds to your garden by making it as attractive to them as possible and to use net and other protection over plants and crops liable to damage. Black cotton put over primroses on a few twiggy sticks just before the buds start to swell will be almost invisible and does not appear to cause the birds, chiefly sparrows, any damage. There is also the rule that the size of a bird population is governed by the food supply available. The more species you encourage, the less food there will be for some of the species which cause the damage and the better the eventual balance.

Many of the most attractive bird species are seed eaters. Wild flowers which will attract them are given in the tables on pages 133–47. Of all the species, teasel is one of the most attractive as goldfinches will feed on the seeds in winter and this will be a bonus for any keen photographer with a good zoom lens. A number of common garden weeds like chickweed, fat-hen, groundsel and shepherd's-purse are a valuable source of food for a number of bird species, so if you leave them in odd corners or on the vegetable plot between crops, you could be surprised and pleased at the visitors who come and feed on them.

The early blooming lesser celandine (*above left*) and germander speedwell (*above right*) enjoy shady sites. For a front-of-border plant the wild strawberry (*below*), which makes good ground cover, is ideal.

Fruits and berries will naturally form an important part of the diet of a number of birds. They will quite often be left until late in the winter when, almost overnight it seems, a flock of the right bird will discover them and the bush or shrub will be stripped. It can give a new interest to a garden to record which bird species take what and when; their individual preferences can be quite surprising.

You will also encourage birds to your garden by providing plenty of song posts and nesting sites. Even a small garden can normally find room for one of two dwarf trees and these can provide quite good bird cover. Where there is more room, a combination of native trees and shrubs like silver birch, rowan, blackthorn, guelder rose, and hawthorn with the rambling dog-rose, traveller's-joy and honeysuckle will all give ideal conditions.

◆ SANCTUARY FOR OTHER ANIMALS ◆

Even more than birds, providing a home for four-legged wildlife in a garden needs some qualification. Few gardens would want to house nesting rabbits, for example, while the intrusion of deer and other large animals can be a disaster – to both cultivated and native plants alike. Even small and apparently harmless creatures like field mice and voles can at times dig up bulbs and damage seeds and seedlings.

However, some small mammals are entirely beneficial in a garden and should be encouraged. The hedgehog, for example, must eat an uncountable number of slugs and snails in a year and once you have a family established, can virtually eliminate the need for slug pellets. Their overall natural population is still quite low, however, so you will need to encourage them to hibernate in your garden over winter by leaving piles of leaves undisturbed in orchards or dry hedge bottoms.

The tall, stately purple-loosestrife (*left*) thrives in a garden's natural wet patch. The bogbean (*right*), with its delicate star-like white flowers enjoys a position at the pond's edge or in shallow waters.

Otherwise they might leave for better quarters elsewhere. When active, hedgehogs are sometimes given saucers of milk left out over night, but this might also encourage the local cats – to which hedgehogs are not very partial.

Moles would be regarded as awful pests in an ornamental lawn or amongst the vegetables but do very little permanent harm in rough grass or a mini-meadow. In fact, the soil they throw up is usually below the level of the grass-cutter blades and makes a good seedbed in which broad-leaved flowers can germinate and so re-generate.

◆ WILDLIFE IN PONDS AND STREAMS ◆

Water wildlife has got more scarce as marshes and ponds are drained and river levels have fallen. Ponds, or better still a stream running through a garden, are alternatives as a place in which to create a balanced water micro-ecology, where plants and other organisms live together in harmony.

It will be necessary to banish any ever-hungry goldfish and other ornamental fishes from a pond, however, even though you feed them, they will still eat frogspawn, larvae and other small insects. The native stickleback will do little harm, or the minnow in a fresh running stream.

Any new pond will be colonised quite quickly by a whole range of water life, and sometimes it is difficult to see where they come from. Dragonflies, water boatmen, pond skaters and several others often arrive almost before the pond has settled down. In spring, toads, frogs and even newts might arrive to lay their spawn, especially if there is other water fairly close. Never take spawn from natural water, even if it appears in abundance, as you might disturb the ecological balance of that particular pond or stream. A jam-jar-full taken from a neighbour's pond is more permissible.

Water plants will also introduce the eggs of a number of species, especially if they are taken from an existing pond and not bought from a more sterile water-plant-raising nursery. This is especially true of the eggs and young of the water-snail, which is essential in any pond to help control the dreaded blanket weed or algae. Another way to bring in eggs and larvae of a wide range of other species is to transfer a bucket of the black ooze from the bottom of another well-established pond and pour it into yours. This will introduce a number of aquatic creatures, hopefully including the delicate damselfly, smaller but equally as beautiful as the dragonfly.

Amphibious creatures will only be attracted to your pond and stay there if given the right conditions. In the first place the pond must be in the right site, fairly protected but not too surrounded by trees which will smother it with leaves in autumn. Toads, newts and frogs need somewhere under which they can hibernate, like nearby logs, stones and other moist places. Frogs will also live in the deep mud at the bottom of a well-established pool. They also need surrounding vegetation like grass or a moist shrub border in summer, where they can hunt for their food of slugs and other small creatures.

Finally, a well-stocked pond will also contain a good balance of plants (see page 40). A water garden is, however, a living thing and like any other part of the garden will need managing if it is to be kept in balance and remain an attractive home for a wide range of species. This involves topping up the evaporated water in dry weather, using soft rainwater if available, raking out blanket-weed until it is controlled naturally and, especially in a small pond, regularly thinning plants to stop them over-growing. Such is the increased interest in ponds nowadays that you should have no problem getting rid of the surplus.

• THE BALANCE OF NATURE •

From a study of the wildlife which you attract to your garden can come a much heightened interest in the balance of nature in general. Despite all the prophets of gloom and doom, the natural world is still a wonderful place. Let there be no doubt, however, it is seriously threatened all over the world, including many parts of our own country. We can do something about it, if only, as suggested in this book, by encouraging wildlife in our million acres of private gardens.

If you want to do more, a list of protection and preservation societies is given on page 151. With the aid of these bodies, or on their own, private citizens can do a great deal to stem some of the destruction which, perhaps inevitably, is the price we often have to pay for progress. Individual action has had surprising success, including some against the most powerfully entrenched organisations.

Some of this has come from realising that, in wildlife terms, there is no longer any barrier between town and countryside. A number of good wildlife parks have now been established in cities and a wide range of plants and animals thrive in the most unlikely urban conditions. As we have been forced to lose much of the countryside, whole new vistas have been opened for wildlife preservation in towns in which parks and gardens play a very important part.

To start by growing a few wild flowers in your garden can therefore lead you on to a new understanding of how the whole natural ecology works and the way that all living creatures should fit into it, including ourselves. From greater understanding can come a wider appreciation of conservation in all aspects; not only whether we should encourage our rich pattern of inherited wildlife, but also how practically to start doing it. Then we shall be able to say justly that we have not merely inherited this land from our forebears, but we have also held it in trust for our successors.

GUIDE TO THE 100 MOST SUITABLE WILDFLOWERS

Any selection of wild flowers suitable to grow as garden plants must be purely arbitrary. So much can depend on soil type, size and type of garden and its situation. There is also the very important matter of personal preference.

This guide to one hundred 'most suitable' wild flowers therefore attempts to select the species which are both interesting and will probably contribute most to your enjoyment. Generally they are also fairly easy to grow and not too aggressive to other plants, and so fit into the average garden. Mention is also made in some entries of other members of the same genus which could be planted as alternatives in some situations; for example, water avens for a mini-marsh in place of wood avens for shade. Similarly, some entries also mention other species useful for growing in the same habitat or where there is another similar link.

In addition to including the ever-popular wild flowers such as primrose, cowslip, sweet violet and oxeye daisy, the selection also describes a number which might not be so well-known to many gardeners. Comprehensive growing instructions are therefore given for all species, using a simple code. This lists their flowering season, preferences for soil type and situation and gives a guide to the ways they can be propagated (for further details see page 24–7).

Both the popular and Latin names given for the plants are in all cases those listed in the 1986 edition of *English Names of Wild Flowers*, published by The Botanical Society of the British Isles. Where there are other popular common names these are also given as alternatives; for example, lady's-smock for cuckooflower.

·AGRIMONY·

Agrimonia eupatoria

Flowering season ◆ **June to August**	
Soil ◆ **normal border**	
Acidity ◆ **neutral/acid**	
Situation ◆ **sun/partial shade**	
Propagation ◆ **seed/division**	

This is a native perennial which grows on road-sides, under hedge banks and along the edges of fields fairly widely in the south but less commonly in the north. Also known as 'church steeples', it has spikes of yellow flowers with a faint scent of apricots and finely divided, attractive foliage.

In good garden soil agrimony will grow to about 60cm (2ft) and makes a pleasant, though not outstandingly colourful, plant for the mixed border. It also grows well in grass, looks most attractive growing above other lower plants in a wild border, and attracts insects.

Hemp-agrimony (*Eupatorium cannabinum*) is an entirely different perennial plant with mauve-pink flowers from a separate family. This grows in damp woods and ditches and in the garden is most useful for the shady side of a pond. It will grow in quite deep shade and is suitable anywhere where the soil is not chalky and stays moist.

Hemp is an imported annual plant and another name for cannabis which must not, of course, be grown in this country except under licence.

Agrimony has a long history of medical treatment against complaints like colds and fevers and as a blood purifier. It also makes a yellow dye.

Agrimony

·BETONY·

Stachys officinalis

Flowering season ◆ **June to September**	
Soil ◆ **normal border**	
Acidity ◆ **alkaline/neutral**	
Situation ◆ **sun/partial shade**	
Propagation ◆ **seed, division**	

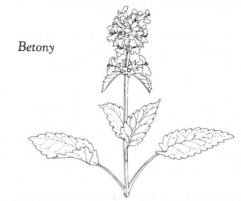

Betony

This is a fairly common plant of woodlands and clearings and is sometimes found in more open meadows and scrub. It is related to the wound-worts and like them was once used for a range of medicinal treatments, including inhalation for bronchitis and as a poultice of the fresh leaves for wounds, bites and poisonous stings. Dried and combined with colt's-foot and eyebright it has also been used as an ingredient of herbal tobacco, in a mixture for snuff and on its own as an infusion for tea.

Betony is a pretty and fairly vigorous perennial with a strong rootstock and its square stems with widely spaced and rather sparse leaves are characteristic of the members of this family. In the garden it grows to a height of about 60cm (2ft) and produces a mass of purple-red blossoms which are very attractive to bees.

In the wild betony grows mostly on lighter soils but in the garden it seems far more tolerant and will even grow on quite heavy clay. It is a most effective plant for the middle of a mixed border but will also thrive in a wild garden in competition with other vigorous plants. Betony will establish well in the grass of a hedge bottom but should only be used in a seed mixture for a mini-meadow on lighter soils.

BLOODY
· CRANE'S-BILL ·

Geranium sanguineum

Flowering season ◆ **May to August**	
Soil ◆ **normal border**	
Acidity ◆ **alkaline**	
Situation ◆ **sun/partial shade**	
Propagation ◆ **seed, scarification advised**	

This beautiful perennial member of a large family is unfortunately quite rare in the wild and only found in parts of northern Britain on rocky limestone, along the coasts and in pastures and woods in the hilly uplands. The name comes from the brilliant magenta colour of the flowers.

Bloody crane's-bill is every bit as worth growing in the garden as many of the related cultivated geraniums, some of which have been developed from it. In good soil it grows to about 45cm (18in) and has a strong rootstock, sending up a mass of shoots and finely-divided, hairy green leaves with the flowers carried singly just above them. Bloody crane's-bill makes a good plant for the front or middle of a mixed flower border and, because of the dense foliage, gives good ground cover. Do not, however, plant it with spring or summer flowering bulbs or it will quickly smother them.

Herb-robert (*G. robertianum*) is a native short-lived perennial member of the geranium family, best treated as an annual. It is nothing like so vigorous as bloody crane's-bill, though growing almost as tall, but makes a neat plant with masses of small, pink flowers and green foliage turning crimson later. It flowers from late spring until late autumn and grows almost anywhere in the garden – and will if allowed to set seed. Herb-robert likes partial shade or sun and looks well under shrubs, in a wild garden where other plants will help keep it under control or to give colour to any untidy corner.

· BLUEBELL ·

Hyacinthoides non-scriptus

Flowering season ◆ **April to June**	
Soil ◆ **normal border**	
Acidity ◆ **acid/neutral**	
Situation ◆ **sun/partial shade**	
Propagation ◆ **division/seed, stratification advised**	

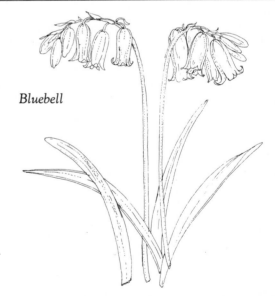

Bluebell

The natural home of bluebells is open woodland, under the light shade of deciduous trees or where they are coppiced. In the summer months they may be completely covered by bracken. In the garden they are very tolerant of soil and site and may be grown either in an open border or in semi-shade. During the summer they will benefit from being shaded by nearby taller, later-flowering herbaceous plants.

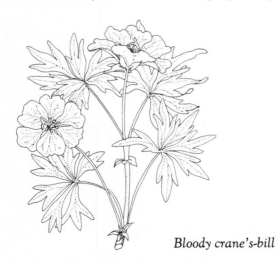

Bloody crane's-bill

As in the wild, bluebells in the border eventually make very large clumps so need regular splitting. Planted in the grass or a wild corner of the garden, possibly at the base of a tree, they need never be disturbed. Bluebells grow to about 50cm (20in). Picking the flowers will not damage the plant but avoid taking more than the odd leaf to add to a flower arrangement. As with all bulbs, avoid trampling the rest of the foliage or cutting it with a mower but leave it to die down naturally.

Most flowers are the traditional bluebell blue, but there are also pink and white forms. Though not often seen in the wild, these are probably not cultivated garden escapes but genuine natural mutations of the original flower. Despite being so widespread in the British Isles, few uses are recorded for the bluebell apart from a starch once made from the bulbs to stiffen Elizabethan ruffles. The sticky juice of the plant, which is actually slightly poisonous, has also been used to make a gum for book-binding.

·BUGLE·

Ajuga reptans

Flowering season ♦ **May to June**	
Soil ♦ **moist**	
Acidity ♦ **neutral/alkaline**	
Situation ♦ **sun, shade, ponds and marsh**	
Propagation ♦ **seed/division**	

Bugle is a very accommodating plant which will grow in either full sun, heavy shade or almost anything in between. In the wild it is a common plant of both woodlands and moist grassland where it forms large masses of purple leaves crowned with deep blue flowers. There are also pink and white flowered forms.

In the garden the abundant foliage of bugle gives helpful ground-hugging cover against weeds, as it spreads rapidly by runners. The flowers grow on a spike to a height of about 25cm (10in) and do not often set seed. It is a very useful plant for the front of a border but can smother other low-growing plants and dwarf spring bulbs unless kept under control. Bugle grows happily on heavy clay, but dislikes dry, light soils, and is a good plant for a

Bugle

mini-marsh, around the edge of ponds or in a moist wild garden. The flowers are a source of nectar for early-flying insects. There are a number of cultivated forms of bugle with different coloured foliage.

Plants which grow well with bugle include two from the same botanical family, ground-ivy (*Glechoma hederacea*) and water mint (*Mentha aquatica*), both liking wet conditions. Despite a rather humdrum name, ground-ivy gives excellent creeping ground cover. It has lighter blue flowers than bugle and blooms earlier in the spring. Water mint is the prettiest of all the native mints and is a true amphibian, growing well either on marshy land or in quite deep water.

Bulbous buttercup

BULBOUS
◆BUTTERCUP◆

Ranunculus bulbosus

Flowering season ◆	**April to June**
Soil ◆	**normal border**
Acidity ◆	**acid/alkaline**
Situation ◆	**sun/partial shade, meadow**
Propagation ◆	**seed/division**

This is one of the large family of buttercups common in fields, lawns and meadows. The name probably came from a long-held belief that the flowers gave colour to butter. Being regarded by many as weeds, farmers and gardeners must have spent, and agrochemical companies made, a small fortune trying to eradicate buttercups. They may win an occasional battle but the buttercups in the end return.

The bulbous buttercup grows generally in drier soil than some of the other common species. It is widespread in grassy places in England and Wales but rather rarer in Scotland and Ireland. The flowers have characteristic sepals turning back towards the petals. In the garden it can make a good inhabitant of a flowering meadow or a dry, grassy bank, where it will flower slightly earlier than other species.

The meadow buttercup (*R. acris*) grows in moister, more fertile soil where the flowering stems can grow up to 90cm (3ft), while the flowers are slightly larger. It likes an irrigated lawn but, with competition from the grasses, will not grow nearly so tall. Regular lawn cutting will often encourage it to flower into the autumn.

Creeping buttercup (*R. repens*) is an indication of poor drainage and wet soil and can be almost impossible to eradicate once established in gardens. In the wild the flowers bring a mass of colour to wet places.

◆CAT'S-EAR◆

Hypochoeris radicata

Flowering season ◆	**May to September**
Soil ◆	**normal border**
Acidity ◆	**neutral**
Situation ◆	**sun, meadow**
Propagation ◆	**seed/division**

This is one of the native 'yellow daisies', often mistaken for the related dandelion and of which the perennial 'cat's-ear', probably so-called from the small leaflets on the stems, is one of the most common. In the wild it is found in meadows, waste

Cat's-ear

places and on roadsides throughout Britain and is often a more widespread weed of established lawns than dandelion.

In the garden cat's-ear will grow to about 60cm (2ft) and with numerous bright yellow flowers throughout the summer, deserves a much better fate than being sprayed or hoed off as a weed. The best place for it is in a flowering meadow or grassy bank, where it mixes well with other meadow flowers and the grasses. It is very attractive as a source of nectar to bees and other insects, especially the hover fly which invariably finds it in late summer.

Rough hawkbit (*Leontodon hispidus*) is another common relation of the dandelion. In the wild this is found on grassy slopes and is common in England but more scattered elsewhere. The stems are usually shorter than cat's-ear but the flower larger and a similar bright yellow. It too grows best in a mini-meadow.

Goat's-beard (*Tragopogon pratensis*), or 'Jack-go-to-bed-by-noon', is a delightful annual member of the family with flowers that open early and close at mid-day. Quite common in the wild, it is another plant for a flowering meadow. The flowers are followed by more attractive 'umbrella' seedheads than dandelion.

Cheddar pink

♦ CHEDDAR PINK ♦

Dianthus gratianopolitanus

Flowering season ♦ June to July	
Soil ♦ poor and dry	
Acidity ♦ neutral/alkaline	
Situation ♦ sun	
Propagation ♦ seed/cutting	

This is one of the native pinks, or dianthus, sometimes very localised in their distribution in the wild but many of which have adapted successfully to garden conditions. This gives opportunity for a wider public to appreciate their benefits and less chance of ecological disturbance at the natural sites.

Cheddar pink is a good example, which grows only in the Cheddar Gorge in Somerset and is now so rare that it is legally a protected plant. The seed

available is of garden origin but it keeps the characteristics of the original plants. These grow to about 20cm (8in) with deep pink, fringed single flowers which are quite large and strongly scented. The plants form small clumps, with blue-green leaves and this is an ideal plant to grow on a sunny rockery or at the front of a well-drained border.

The distribution of Deptford pink (*D. armeria*) is not quite so limited but is confined mainly to roadsides, dry grassland and hedges in the south of England and is still quite rare. It grows very erect up to about 45cm (18in), is biennial and likes dry, light soil and plenty of sun. The flowers are pink to crimson, are carried on long stems and bloom in July and August.

Maiden pink (*D. deltoides*) is scattered throughout Britain, mainly on dry grasslands, and is again quite rare. The name is said to come from the pink of a maiden's blush. It grows a little taller than Cheddar pink and the plants make a looser mat. The flowers are not so large, mainly pink but can be white or crimson and there are a number of cultivated forms. Like almost all dianthus, it likes good drainage and sun and is an ideal plant for the rock garden. It flowers from July to September.

CLUSTERED
◆ BELLFLOWER ◆
Campanula glomerata

Flowering season ◆ **May to September**	
Soil ◆ **poor and dry**	
Acidity ◆ **neutral/alkaline**	
Situation ◆ **sun**	
Propagation ◆ **seed/division**	

A very colourful member of the large campanula family, growing in the wild on chalk downlands, mainly in the south and east of England. It carries clusters of purplish-blue flowers at the end of very erect stems, which are also covered with a mass of serrated, dark green leaves. A number of cultivated forms are now grown in gardens, with colours ranging from white to deep violet.

Like many of the campanulas, clustered bellflower grown in good, well-drained border soil can be quite vigorous. Although it only grows to a height of about 45cm (18in), it makes a large clump quite quickly which, without competition, can be very invasive and will need frequent thinning. A better site might be in a sunny corner or on a rockery, where it will grow less tall but lose nothing of the beauty of the flowers.

Nettle-leaved bellflower (*C. trachelium*), often called 'bats-in-the-belfry', grows about twice as tall and, coming from the woodlands, prefers more shade and moisture. Growing up to 75cm (30in) this is a good plant for the rear of a mixed border, where it is not so invasive as clustered bellflower. The flowers are slightly more lilac but mainly carried singly on flowering spikes and not in a cluster, though plants can vary in colour and shape.

Giant bellflower (*C. latifolia*) is our largest native campanula and has been grown in gardens for many years. The true wild plant has mid-blue or white flowers.

◆ COLUMBINE ◆
Aquilegia vulgaris

Flowering season ◆ **May to June**	
Soil ◆ **normal border**	
Acidity ◆ **alkaline/neutral**	
Situation ◆ **sun/partial shade**	
Propagation ◆ **seed**	

'Granny's-bonnet' and 'culverwort' are two other names given to the columbine, which is now quite rare in the wild but has survived since at least the sixteenth century in cottage gardens. The generic name *aquilegia* refers to the resemblance between the spurs on the flowers and the talons of an eagle. Modern cultivated hybrid aquilegias have larger flowers with longer spurs, come in many different colours and grow up to 90cm (3ft) tall. Even in good soil, the native columbine will only grow to a maximum of 60cm (2ft). It has smaller blue flowers, but far more of them and will seed all over the garden if allowed. In the process it cross-breeds quite happily with the more colourful garden varieties.

Even without the flowers, the pretty blue-green foliage, tinged with pink in early spring, makes the

Clustered bellflower

columbine worth a place in any garden border. It likes full sun but can also look most effective in partial shade and with a background of shrub foliage. Columbines can also add colour to a north-facing border but the flowers are rather short-lived and other plants are needed to carry on for the rest of the summer. The green seed-heads are also rather attractive.

Although the columbine plant is poisonous, it was used as a gargle for sore throats and mouths, as a lotion for rheumatism and for the treatment of ulcers. The seeds are also poisonous and when crushed make a potent garden insecticide.

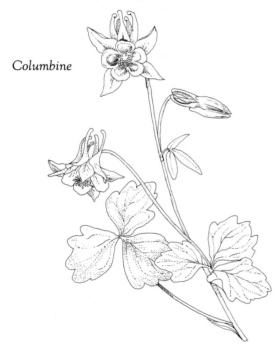

Columbine

COMMON BIRD'S-FOOT-
· TREFOIL ·

Lotus corniculatus

Flowering season ◆ **May to September**	
Soil ◆ **poor and dry**	
Acidity ◆ **acid/alkaline**	
Situation ◆ **sun, meadow**	
Propagation ◆ **seed, scarification advised, division**	

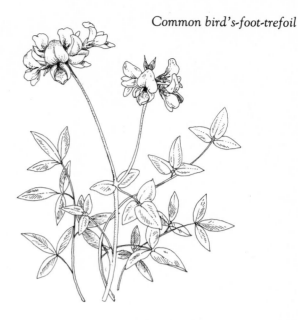

Common bird's-foot-trefoil

This is a good ornamental representative of the clover family to grow in the garden. It has a number of local common and often picturesque names such as 'bacon-and-eggs', 'boots-and-shoes' and 'hop-o'-my-thumb' – over 70 have been recorded. Many of them allude to the colour and distinctive shape of the flowers and the form of the later dense black seed pods. The flowers are yellow with orange or brown tints and have crimson-red buds before they open. They provide colour for most of the summer.

When established bird's-foot-trefoil forms a dense, creeping mat 2½–5cm(1–2in) high and reaching 60cm (2ft) across. The flowers are about 1.2cm (½in) across and they are carried in heads of two to six, followed by attractive black seed pods about 2.5cm (1in) long which, because of the length of flowering, provide a contrast to the later blossoms. Bird's-foot-trefoil is a food plant for the caterpillars of the common blue butterfly and very attractive to bees. Partly for this reason, it is a very useful flower for the mini-meadow or to grow in rough grass but it is also very effective towards the front of a wild flower border.

Other good members of the same family include the creeping common restharrow (*Ononis repens*) which grows to a similar size but has bright pink flowers, and sainfoin (*Onobrychis viciifolia*), a rather taller and bushy plant, with pink flowers streaked with red carried on cone-shaped spikes and also very attractive to bees.

Common comfrey

COMMON
·COMFREY·

Symphytum officinale

Flowering season ◆ May to September	
Soil ◆ moist	
Acidity ◆ neutral	
Situation ◆ sun/partial shade, ponds and marsh	
Propagation ◆ seed/division	

In the wild, comfrey colonises large moist areas of ditches and alongside ponds, streams and rivers. Alternative names such as 'knitbone', 'boneset' and 'bruisewort' come from a range of medical uses, including the treatment of swellings, sprains, broken bones and bruises. It was also used to stem bleeding, whilst added to the bath water it was said to restore virginity. The mineral-rich leaves are still recommended as a valuable ingredient in garden composts, for mulching and to make liquid fertilizer. Russian comfrey is an import with larger and coarser leaves and has naturalized in some parts of the country. There are also some hybrid intermediate forms.

For the garden, comfrey is a very vigorous plant which grows to a height of about 1.2m (4ft) in good soil and, like horse-radish, once planted is almost impossible to eradicate. It is therefore best kept to a corner in a shady and damp part of the garden,

where it will be more controllable. The flowers are borne in profusion for a large part of the summer; most are white and cream but they also shade to blue and pink. It is not really a satisfactory plant for small gardens.

Lungwort (*Pulmonaria officinalis*) is a close relative of comfrey which grows in shady places and makes a good ground cover. Although not a true native, it has naturalised in woods and hedge bottoms and is also widely grown in gardens. With spotted leaves, pink flowers and a much smaller habit, it is a much better plant than comfrey for the mixed border.

COMMON
·DOG-VIOLET·

Viola riviniana

Flowering season ◆ April to July	
Soil ◆ normal border	
Acidity ◆ acid/alkaline	
Situation ◆ partial shade	
Propagation ◆ seed/cuttings/division	

This is the common violet of woodlands, heaths and hedges throughout Britain. It should not be confused with the dog-tooth violet, an imported member of the lily family from Europe also known as 'adder's-tongue', mainly cultivated but sometimes found in the wild as a garden escape.

Common dog-violet

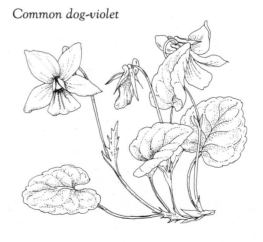

The prefix 'dog' indicates a virtual lack of perfume. Otherwise dog-violet is just as good a plant as the sweet violet, tolerates more shade, grows in larger clumps to about 20cm (8in) in height, and flowers for a longer period. The flowers are violet-blue but a separate species growing on heaths is paler, as is another which flowers much earlier in spring. They also hybridise freely with each other and this makes identification difficult.

Although dog-violets will grow in sun, their flowers are always seen at their best in semi-shade, especially as they flower on into the stronger light of early summer. They are tolerant of most soils and will grow happily in poor soil under trees, provided peat or leaf mould has been incorporated into it. They will also establish a flowering carpet on a grassy, shady bank provided the grass is not allowed to grow too long.

The dog-violet is a food plant for the caterpillars of the fritillary butterflies. The flowers were included in a fourteenth-century recipe for ground rice pudding flavoured with cream and almonds and they had a number of other culinary uses, mostly to add flavour or colour.

COMMON
◆ FUMITORY ◆
Fumaria officinalis

Flowering season ◆ **May to October**	
Soil ◆ **normal border**	
Acidity ◆ **acid/alkaline**	
Situation ◆ **sun**	
Propagation ◆ **seed**	

This is the most garden-worthy small member of the fairly large fumitory family. A native annual, it grows widely on cultivated and waste land and is often one of the first plants to re-colonise a disturbed grass verge on a sunny roadside or building site.

Other members of the species include ramping fumitory (*F. capreolata*) which is much larger and more rare and grows mostly near the sea; wall fumitory (*F. muralis*) growing mainly in walls and at the base of hedges, and the trailing small

fumitory (*F. parviflora*) only found on chalk in the south of England. An alternative name for common fumitory is 'earth smoke', probably from the hazy appearance of a mass of flowers. The yellow fumitory of gardens is more properly called corydalis. This is an import, though now widely naturalised, with a leaf like a maidenhair fern.

On garden soil common fumitory grows to about 45cm (18in). It is decorative with pink or purple tubular flowers tinged crimson carried on spikes and coarse rather fern-like leaves. Although it can be placed at the front of a sunny border, it is probably better seen in a mass in front of a hedge or a rougher part of the garden. If allowed to seed it will spread rapidly to other parts of the garden but is very easy to keep under control.

Though widespread, common fumitory appears to have had no culinary uses, but it was used medically for digestive disorders and as a treatment against disorders of the skin.

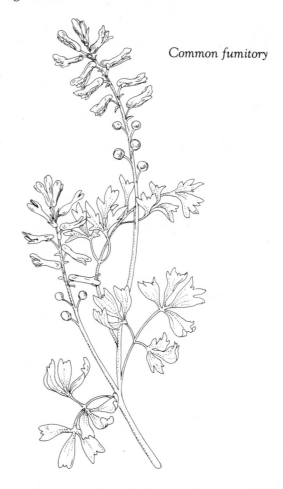

Common fumitory

COMMON
·POPPY·

Papaver rhoeas

Flowering season ◆ **May to September**	
Soil ◆ **normal border**	
Acidity ◆ **acid/alkaline**	
Situation ◆ **sun, meadow**	
Propagation ◆ **seed**	

Immortalised by John McCrae as the scarlet poppy of Flanders fields worn for each Remembrance Day, this is undoubtedly one of the most persistent and widespread of all our British annual wild flowers. Once a weed of cornfields but now effectively controlled by modern herbicides, the seed lasts an incredible length of time in the soil. One missed bout of spraying or soil disturbance during building and road construction and the field poppy will burst out again in all its glory. Records show it germinating on sites previously covered by buildings after possibly two hundred years and it is still a common flower of waste places.

The field poppy is increasingly popular in the garden, both grown in a mixed border of annual wild flowers and as a constituent of a mixture for a

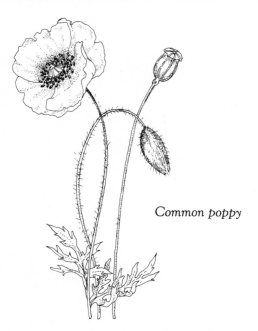

Common poppy

flowering meadow to provide 'first year' colour. In good soil it will grow to 60cm (2ft) tall and the buds, flowers and attractive seed pods all present together makes it a very colourful plant. Stems containing all three can be used for flower arrangement, but the stem bottoms need dipping in boiling water for a minute after picking to prevent wilting. Sow in August–September for flowers the following May; in early spring for flowers in July–August, or in early June for flowers in August–September.

When ripe, the seeds of the field poppy can be shaken out of the seed heads, dried and sprinkled on top of bread, rolls and biscuits. They have also been used in the past mixed with honey as a dressing for cooked fruit. The seeds and flower petals made an ancient remedy against inflamed throats and coughs.

COMMON
·QUAKING-GRASS·

Briza media

Flowering season ◆ **June to August**	
Soil ◆ **normal border**	
Acidity ◆ **neutral/alkaline**	
Situation ◆ **sun/partial shade, meadow**	
Propagation ◆ **seed**	

This native perennial grass used to be common in old grass meadows and on chalky downlands throughout the country, but is now harder to find in the wild and mostly confined to less frequented hillsides. There is also an annual greater quaking-grass (*B. maxima*) quite commonly grown in gardens with larger seedheads used for drying, but this is a native of mediterranean regions. Lesser quaking-grass (*B. minor*) is also annual and seen on roadsides in south-west England.

Quaking grass has attractive purplish-green flowers, followed by roughly diamond-shaped seedheads carried on slender stems which 'quake' in the wind. It is worth growing in small clumps as a feature plant in a mixed border where it will grow to about 60cm (2ft). Quaking grass makes an attractive addition to a grass sward, when it will probably only grow half as high. It likes sun but will also grow in partial shade under high cover.

Sheep's-fescue (*Festuca ovina*) is another native perennial from a large family of fine-leaved grasses. It still grows widely on heaths and moorlands but many of the sheep-grazed downlands which gave the name are now either ploughed or seeded with more productive grasses. In recent years it has become popular as a feature grass for gardens, and there is a cultivated and blue-leaved form known in seed lists as *Festuca ovina glauca.* The native sheep's-fescue is also blueish with finely rolled leaves. It grows to about 30cm (12in) grown in clumps in the border but rather less in a grass mixture.

Common quaking-grass

COMMON
·RESTHARROW·

Ononis repens

Flowering season ◆ **June to September**

Soil ◆ **poor and dry**

Acidity ◆ **neutral/alkaline**

Situation ◆ **sun, meadow**

Propagation ◆ **seed, scarification advised/cuttings**

A delicate-pink flowering member of the vetch family, this native shrubby perennial grows widely in meadows and other grassy places on light soil throughout much of Britain but is rare in Scotland. The name restharrow came from the difficulty in cutting through the tough and matted roots when cultivating land. Another name for it is 'cammock', from a taint given to milk and butter by cows grazing on the plants. Spiny restharrow is a slightly shorter and more prickly plant growing mainly in southern and eastern England on chalky soils.

Common restharrow grows to just over 30cm (12in) in height but with sprawling stems up to 60cm (2ft) long. As these root into the soil at every joint, a single plant can cover a large space quite quickly. It is therefore not a good plant for a flower border but looks best in a mixed wild flower garden. It also makes a good plant for a flowering meadow and is tolerant of salt conditions at the seaside.

The flowers are bright pink at the tips fading towards the base. It blooms for much of the summer and although the flowers have no perfume, the leaves are scented. Common restharrow is attractive to butterflies and is a food plant of the common blue. The tough roots were once dug up and chewed by children, which gave another name of wild liquorice, actually a different plant altogether, or 'Spanish root'. At one time shoots were also eaten either raw or cooked and it is said to be a favourite plant of goats.

Common restharrow

COMMON
◆ ROCK-ROSE ◆

Helianthemum nummularium

Flowering season ◆ **May to August**	
Soil ◆ **normal border**	
Acidity ◆ **neutral/alkaline**	
Situation ◆ **sun, meadow**	
Propagation ◆ **seed, stratification advised, scarification advised/cuttings**	

This native sub-shrub is common throughout much of Britain on chalky soils in meadows, scrubland and on hills and mountains. Despite the name, it is not related to the rose but grows in sunny positions and flowers for much of the summer. Other common names for the rock-rose are 'sun-rose' and 'beauty-of-the-sun'.

The flowers of the rock-rose are usually bright yellow with darker stamens but there are also lighter forms, including some cream and almost white. Unfortunately they only hold their petals for a day. Despite this short life, the flowers are produced in great numbers on stems rambling over the soil making it a good plant for the garden.

In good soil rock-rose grows to a maximum of 30cm (12in) but often less, which makes it suitable for the rock garden, in the crevices of a paved path or the front of a sunny border. It responds to hard pruning of the rambling stems back to the main plant immediately after flowering ceases. The rock-rose will also grow well on a dry, grassy bank or a mini-meadow on poor soil.

The garden cultivated many-coloured forms of helianthemum have all been developed from the wild rock-rose. It is also fairly closely related to the garden cistus, not a native but coming from warmer climes and also commonly mis-named the rock-rose. Like all the family, our native rock-rose is probably easiest to propagate from cuttings of shoots taken in summer.

Common rock-rose

COMMON
◆ ST JOHN'S-WORT ◆

Hypericum perforatum

Flowering season ◆ **June to September**	
Soil ◆ **normal border**	
Acidity ◆ **acid/alkaline**	
Situation ◆ **sun/partial shade**	
Propagation ◆ **seed/division**	

St John's-wort is the most widespread native example of a fairly large group of herbaceous and semi-shrubby plants, which includes the ubiquitous cultivated rose-of-sharon (*H. calycinum*). Named after St John the Baptist, the plant may have featured in ceremonies connected with the saint's day on 24 June, when it is in full flower. It was also used medically, including making an oil to soothe cuts and sprains and as a tea drunk to cure insomnia and coughs.

In the wild common St John's-wort grows in the hedgerows, woodlands and on grassy banks. Other relatives like the hairy and the marsh St John's-wort prefer more moist conditions, whilst there is a trailing species widely found on acid heathland.

For the garden it makes a bushy plant about 60cm (2ft) tall with erect stems and bearing pointed leaves marked with translucent dots – which gives the Latin name to the species. The bright yellow, five-petalled flowers are about 2.5cm (1in) in size and have a mass of long and very

Common St John's-wort

Common toadflax

prominent yellow stamens. This makes it a very attractive garden plant, especially as yellow can be lacking in the border later in the season. Common St John's-wort spreads quite vigorously, however, by underground rhizomes and to avoid having to frequently lift and divide it, a better place might be in a hedge bottom or on a grassy bank. It does not smother weeds so well as the rose-of-sharon but is a much brighter looking plant, though with smaller flowers, and does not carry the same sort of rather tired looking foliage over winter.

COMMON ◆ TOADFLAX ◆

Linaria vulgaris

Flowering season ◆ June to October	
Soil ◆ normal border	
Acidity ◆ neutral/alkaline	
Situation ◆ sun	
Propagation ◆ seed/division	

A pretty plant for the garden it is related to the cultivated annual *Linaria* grown as a border edging. Toadflax is taller and grows to 60cm (2ft) in

good soil. The long-spurred flowers are bright yellow with orange centres, not unlike a snapdragon in shape, which gave the country name of 'butter and eggs'. It was used as a diuretic and purgative and was said to be good for cleaning the liver. When boiled with lard it was used in an ointment for treating ulcers, sores, piles and inflamed eyes.

In the wild toadflax grows very widely in open woodlands, waste places, roadsides and even cultivated land. It will grow very well in a mixed garden border but, as a born survivor, it can be invasive unless surrounded by other equally aggressive flowers. Toadflax is best planted as a clump on a grassy bank or on the edge of a wild garden, where the bright yellow of the flowers and the bushy green foliage can be seen at their best. It is a good supplier of nectar for bumble bees and a food plant for the spotted fritillary caterpillar.

Ivy-leaved toadflax (*Cymbalaria muralis*) is a fairly close relative, but not really a native. It was probably introduced here early in the seventeenth century and is now widely naturalised. It has lilac-coloured flowers with pink centres and glossy small ivy-like leaves and is invaluable for trailing over sunny walls and in a rock garden. There is also a white form. It blooms slightly earlier than common toadflax and is a good nectar plant for bees.

Corn chamomile

CORN
·CHAMOMILE·

Anthemis arvensis

Flowering season ◆ **June to July**	
Soil ◆ **normal border/poor and dry**	
Acidity ◆ **neutral**	
Situation ◆ **sun**	
Propagation ◆ **seed**	

There is often some confusion between a number of white daisy-like wild flowers, all of which look rather similar. Corn chamomile used to be a common annual weed of corn and is closely related to the much harder to find perennial chamomile (*Chamaemelum nobile*), which itself has a non-flowering form called treneague used as an alternative to grass for lawns. The so-called wild chamomile should really be called scented may-weed whereas the stinking mayweed, still a very common weed of cultivated land, is really a chamomile. All totally confusing!

The chamomiles have long been favourites with herbalists and the ways they have been used are innumerable. Chamomile herb tea is widely available commercially and makes a very pleasantly aromatic drink, claimed to cure headaches, 'nerves', insomnia and digestive disorders. They have been used in anti-allergic cosmetics and as a bright yellow dye obtained after boiling the plants.

Corn chamomile is a very bright garden plant and the flowers last well when picked for a mixed floral decoration. As an annual plant it can only be grown from seed, but it self-sets well and in the right situation seldom needs re-sowing. The best way to grow it is in a mixed annual bed with others like field poppy and corn marigold, sowing each in defined areas rather than as an overall mixture. In garden soil it will grow to only about 30cm (12in) tall so needs keeping to the front of a border.

·CORNCOCKLE·

Agrostemma githago

Flowering season ◆ **June to August**	
Soil ◆ **normal border**	
Acidity ◆ **neutral/acid**	
Situation ◆ **sun**	
Propagation ◆ **seed**	

An alternative name for this purple-pink annual wild flower is corn campion, as it rather resembles other campions and is in the same botanical family. This is not a true native but because it became such a widespread weed of cereals and arable land, it has every right to be regarded as one. When it was found that the poisonous seeds were a dangerous contaminant of flour it was gradually eliminated and now is very hard to find in the wild.

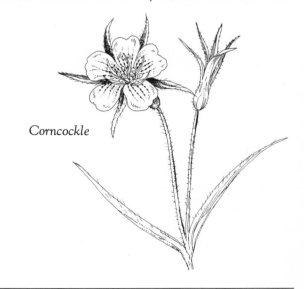

Corncockle

Corncockle is an annual plant but seeds itself prolifically. As the seeds are quite large, there is very little risk of them being spread by the wind or other means back into the countryside and annoying local farmers. It can grow up to 1.2m (4ft) tall in good garden soil without competition and needs putting against a fence or in with other plants to support it – as in a cornfield. This is, in fact, one wild flower which grows better when mixed with other annuals than in a clump on its own.

The vivid flowers of corncockle are complemented by an attractive five-toothed calyx, giving them a rather starfish-like effect, while the seed heads which follow are also striking and worth drying for winter decoration. Like the campions, corncockle has rather greyish-green foliage which is due to a covering of fine, white hairs.

Although the seeds are poisonous, the leaves were once pickled with bacon and it is also used for homeopathic medicine.

◆ CORNFLOWER ◆

Centaurea cyanus

Flowering season ◆ **June to August**	
Soil ◆ **normal border**	
Acidity ◆ **neutral/acid**	
Situation ◆ **sun**	
Propagation ◆ **seed**	

'Corn bluebottle' was another country name given to this one-time widespread weed of the cornfields, while the ability of the tough, wiry stems to blunt the scythe blades of harvesters produced the other title of 'hurt sickle'. Most flowers in the wild were the typical cornflower blue but occasional purple, white and pink forms were subsequently selected for garden use. A double blue variety has also been grown for many years as a popular commercial cut flower. The shorter, leafier and larger-flowered perennial cornflower is seen in the wild in some areas as a garden escape.

Cornflowers will grow anywhere in the garden where there is sun but they dislike a chalky soil. In good soil they grow to about 90cm (3ft) tall but although reasonably robust, they will need supporting in windy weather. This can be provided

either by twiggy sticks placed around the growing plants when they are young, or mixing with field poppy to give natural support. Dead-heading will prolong the flowering season and as the first plants to flower are those which self-seed and start growing in the autumn, another sowing in spring will give flowers for later in the summer.

All cornflowers are good nectar plants for bees and can also attract a cloud of several sorts of butterflies. They also make an excellent cut flower, while the unopened buds can be preserved by drying or dipping in clear varnish.

Cornflower

◆ CORN MARIGOLD ◆

Chrysanthemum segetum

Flowering season ◆ **June to August**	
Soil ◆ **normal border/poor and dry**	
Acidity ◆ **neutral/acid**	
Situation ◆ **sun**	
Propagation ◆ **seed**	

One of the loveliest of the annual wild flowers and well worth a place in any garden, this is more like a single yellow chrysanthemum than either the pot or other cultivated forms of marigold. Another old country name is yellow oxeye daisy, to which it is quite closely related.

Corn marigold is not a true native but had been established long enough by the fourteenth century for tenant farmers to be ordered to remove it from fields of barley. Nowadays it has been completely eradicated from cornfields but can still be found occasionally on road verges on the mainly lighter soils.

In the garden corn marigold will grow up to 60cm (2ft) under good conditions but rather less on poor, dry soil. It is very free-flowering, much more so than most of the cultivated marigolds, and if the many-branched stems are kept dead-headed it will keep blooming into the autumn. The lemon-yellow flowers contrast very well with most other plants in a mixed border, or it can be grown with poppy, corn chamomile and cornflower in a mixed annual collection. It may not self-seed as well as some other annual wild flowers, so might need a yearly spring sowing to ensure its survival.

Corn marigold blooms are slightly fragrant, long-lasting and make a good cut flower; it is a good nectar plant for the smaller insects. The young leaves have been eaten in the past as a vegetable.

Corn marigold

◆ COWSLIP ◆

Primula veris

Flowering season ◆ **April to May**	
Soil ◆ **normal border**	
Acidity ◆ **neutral/alkaline**	
Situation ◆ **sun/partial shade**	
Propagation ◆ **seed/division**	

The cowslip was once a widespread meadowland flower mainly in lowland Britain for many centuries, now it has become harder to find in the wild, but is an increasingly popular garden plant. Farming practices and possibly over-picking, even transplanting, may have hastened the decline. Although perennial, the plants are short-lived and need to be left to re-generate by self-seeding.

Also known by the almost equally popular name of 'paigles', cowslip is very tolerant of most situations but dislikes acid soils. The bright golden flowers marked with orange are best seen at the front of a border in the spring sunshine, but it will also grow well in semi-shade. The pale green leaves form a rosette up to 20cm (8in) long. The flowers are borne in one-sided clusters of ten to thirty on a stem which grows to about 25cm (10in) high. Cowslip is a very popular ingredient of a seed mixture for a flowering mini-meadow and likes rough grass, provided it is not cut until the seeds are set in about late July.

Cowslip

Equally widely known by the alternative name of lady's smock, this native wild flower blooms over the period covered by the annual visit of the cuckoo. It is the prettiest member of the large cress family, some of which can be eaten while others are rather pernicious weeds of cultivated plants. The colourful annual and perennial forms of cultivated candytuft are also fairly closely related.

In the wild, cuckooflower grows in damp meadows and alongside streams throughout Britain, though it seems most common in the north and west of the country. The typical crucifer-like flowers are carried in bunches and bloom in succession; the colour varies from almost pure white to pinky-lilac with darker lilac veins.

In the garden the cuckooflower grows to about 60cm (2ft) but needs plenty of moisture. It is probably seen at its best growing in pond margins and other wet spots, where it can spread very rapidly by self-seeding, but it also makes a good plant for moist borders, especially when planted in clumps. A planting in a moist, rough grass meadow can also look most effective. It is very easy to propagate by leaf cuttings taken in summer or by division of the plants in the autumn.

Cuckoo flower is attractive to bees, other insects and as a food plant for both the larvae and adults of the early-flying orange-tip butterfly.

Oxlip (*P. elatior*) is a close relative, which was only identified as a separate species in the last century. It has larger, paler yellow flowers than the cowslip without the orange markings and with a scent reminiscent of apricots. In the wild it grows in moist conditions and prefers semi-shade such as coppiced woodlands to open meadows. Oxlip flowers a little later than cowslip so does not cross-hybridise with it as easily as primrose. Distribution in the wild is confined to parts of Essex and East Anglia.

Both cowslips and oxlips are valuable early sources of nectar for insects.

◆ CUCKOOFLOWER ◆

Cardamine pratensis

Flowering season ◆ **April to July**	
Soil ◆ **moist**	
Acidity ◆ **neutral/alkaline**	
Situation ◆ **sun/partial shade, meadow, ponds and marshes**	
Propagation ◆ **seed/cuttings**	

Cuckooflower

Daisy

·DAISY·

Bellis perennis

Flowering season ◆ March to September	
Soil ◆ normal border	
Acidity ◆ acid/alkaline	
Situation ◆ sun, meadow	
Propagation ◆ seed/division	

A member of the largest botanical family, the little perennial meadow daisy flowers for a longer period than almost any other wild flower. Still loved by young children for their daisy-chains, this is a flower that can still be picked safely without risk of it becoming exterminated. Although its name is said to come from 'day's-eye', the flowers only actually open when the weather is bright and the sun shining. Other common names are 'bairnwort', probably another reference to daisy-chains, and 'bruisewort' because of its use in the past to treat aches and bruises.

The wild daisy of lawns and meadows has a single row of white ray petals tinged with pink surrounding a central yellow disc. The plants produce numerous solitary flowers on stems generally not more than 6cm (2½in) high. It is from this that the larger coloured cultivated forms of bellis have been selected. These are very popular grown as 'biennial' bedding to plant with wallflowers and polyanthus in autumn to flower in the following spring. Although colourful and very hardy bedding plants, the flowers seldom seem to have the charm of the original daisy. They are also stronger and if left to seed they can invade a lawn and take over from the weaker wild daisy.

Although in early gardens the daisy was planted as border edging, the best place for it is undoubtedly in grass, leaving it undisturbed in a lawn, or sowing or planting it in rough grass and flowering meadows. The daisy also grows well in the cracks of a garden path and withstands treading. The flowers of daisies provide nectar for butterflies and other insects.

·DANDELION·

Taraxacum officinale

Flowering season ◆ May to August	
Soil ◆ normal border	
Acidity ◆ acid/alkaline	
Situation ◆ sun	
Propagation ◆ seed/division	

Dandelion

This is a perennial native so widespread throughout the country that it barely needs any description. Closely related to the hawkbits, the dandelion grows almost anywhere there is sun but is most commonly found in meadows, cultivated field edges, along the roadside and on waste places. There is also a red-veined species found in marshes. It grows to 35cm (14in) in height. It is one of the most common weeds of lawns but is less often such a problem in cultivated parts of the garden. A host of other country names include 'fairy-clocks', 'shepherd's-clock', 'wishes' and 'Irish daisy'.

Were it not a weed of lawns, dandelion might well be a more popular plant, as it has so much in its favour. The bright yellow flowers are one of the first to come out and the last to fade and very attractive to bees and other insects. The fluffy seedheads are a delight to children and it has a number of medicinal and culinary uses. The dandelion makes an almost indispensable ingredient of a flowering meadow.

Dandelion leaves are a useful addition to a salad and can be picked for most months of the year. The leaves can also be blanched like chicory by covering the plant with a flower pot. The dried roots make a caffeine-free substitute for coffee and in some countries are cooked fresh as a vegetable, while the flowers make a well-known home-made wine. Taken generously, the wine demonstrates why the dandelion was once used medically for urinary disorders. This is reflected in its French name *pissenlit* and some equally expressive local names in English.

◆ DEVIL'S-BIT ◆
SCABIOUS

Succisa pratensis

Flowering season ◆ June to October	
Soil ◆ normal border/moist	
Acidity ◆ acid/alkaline	
Situation ◆ partial shade/meadow	
Propagation ◆ seed/division	

This native perennial is common in marshes, wet meadows and damp woodlands throughout most of Britain. The name comes from medieval folk-

Devil's-bit scabious

lore, which said the devil bit through the root in anger at the Virgin Mary, giving the characteristic shortened rootstock. Most of the pin-cushion shaped flowers are mauve, but with some pink variations, and are carried in great profusion. The leaves are hairy and rounded and the large number of stems make the devil's-bit scabious more of a bush than other native species.

Devil's-bit prefers rather moister soil than other scabious and will grow in more shady conditions. In good soil it reaches 75–90cm (30–36in) and can be planted at the back of a shady border, where it also suppresses weeds. Despite forming a bush, in exposed situations the flowering stems need support and here it might be better grown in a wild garden, using other plants to hold it up. Devil's-bit also likes rough grass and can be an ingredient of a mini-flowering meadow. Sheep's-bit is a much smaller and lilac-blue scabious which can be useful for a rockery or very exposed garden.

Like all the native scabious, and much better than the cultivated imported species, devil's-bit is very useful for attracting a large number of different butterflies and bees, especially late in the summer and into autumn. It is also a food plant for the marsh fritillary, rarely seen in gardens. The very large seedheads, technically called achenes, are attractive in late autumn to seed-eating birds.

◆ DOG-ROSE ◆
Rosa canina

Flowering season ◆ **June to July**	
Soil ◆ **normal border**	
Acidity ◆ **neutral**	
Situation ◆ **sun, partial shade**	
Propagation ◆ **seed, stratification advised**	

This native species of rose is widespread in hedgerows and open woodland throughout lowland Britain. It is also very variable in growth and the flowers can be pink or white. Though rather short-lived, they are followed by the well-known flask-shaped scarlet hips in autumn, still widely made into syrup as a valuable source of vitamin C.

The sweet-briar (*R. rubiginosa*), or 'eglantine', is another native less common than the dog-rose and growing mainly on chalky soils. It also grows slightly smaller, has darker pink petals and small, rounded and perfumed leaves. Both of these roses were parents of the original shrub roses, ancestors themselves of the modern hybrids of today.

In good garden soil the dog-rose grows up to 3m (10ft) tall and produces a thicket of arching stems with rather fearsome prickles. Following the old garden saying that 'growth follows the knife', the

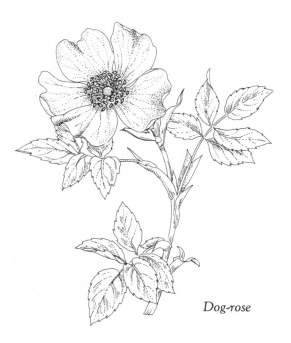

Dog-rose

dog-rose usually responds to pruning by becoming even more vigorous. It is therefore best grown in one of the wilder corners of the garden, where it can be left undisturbed to settle down and form quite a well-behaved climbing shrub providing masses of flowers and hips and a good home for birds and small mammals.

In addition to making syrup, the seeds from rose hips have long been used by children as an itching powder, while the flower petals add colour to salads and scent to pot-pourri, rose water and cosmetics.

◆ FEVERFEW ◆
Tanacetum parthenium

Flowering season ◆ **July to August**	
Soil ◆ **normal border**	
Acidity ◆ **neutral**	
Situation ◆ **sun**	
Propagation ◆ **seed/division**	

So much has been written in recent years about the benefits of feverfew to control migraine, that it must now be one of our most widely planted garden herbs. Not a true native, it was introduced from Europe many years ago and is now very widely distributed throughout the country.

In the wild the daisy-like flowers of feverfew are found on walls, roadsides, waste places and under sunny hedgerows, where it spreads very prolifically. The light green and rather feathery foliage has a pungent smell when crushed, like another close relative the pyrethrum.

In the garden and on good soil feverfew makes a small bush growing up to 60cm (2ft) tall and covered with white flowers in late summer. These are attractive to some insects but the pungent smell appears to repel bees. For the rest of the year the light green foliage remains attractive, even during winter. Feverfew sets seed readily so the flowers must be dead-headed if it is not to plant itself, literally, all over the garden. It can be grown as a border edging on poor soil, where it can be clipped to keep it in shape after flowering. It is probably best in a herb collection and it also thrives in pots and other containers.

Feverfew

In addition to eating the leaves to relieve migraine or rheumatic and arthritic pain, an infusion of feverfew has been used against digestive complaints and mixed with honey as a cough cure.

·FIELD SCABIOUS·

Knautia arvensis

Flowering season ◆ **June to September**	
Soil ◆ **normal border**	
Acidity ◆ **neutral/alkaline**	
Situation ◆ **sun, meadow**	
Propagation ◆ **seed, division**	

This is a fairly common native perennial wild flower inhabiting chalky, dry grassland, roadsides and waste places throughout Britain except in northern Scotland. The most attractive part of the field scabious is the pin-cushion-like, lilac-mauve flowerhead, which is made up of over 50 individual flowers. An alternative name is 'gypsy-rose'.

The closely related small scabious (*Scabiosa columbaria*) is not so widespread and grows mainly on chalk downlands and meadows in southern England. It is shorter, more branched and the flowers are more delicately coloured. The name scabious comes from the past use of this family for the treatment of scabies.

In the garden field scabious grows to 90cm (3ft) and although it can make a very handsome border plant, is probably best grown as an ingredient of a flowering meadow, especially on light, well-drained soil. Although small scabious can also be grown in a meadow, as it usually reaches about 30cm (12in) and is shorter and more compact, it is a better species for a mixed border. If cut down quite hard after flowering, it frequently produces a second crop of flowers quite late in autumn.

Both types of scabious are excellent plants to grow for bees and butterflies, which they attract in great numbers. The large seeds are very attractive to a number of birds. Another medical treatment was in a mixture with borax and samphire against pimples, freckles and dandruff.

Field scabious

◆ FOXGLOVE ◆

Digitalis purpurea

Flowering season ◆ June to September	
Soil ◆ moist	
Acidity ◆ acid	
Situation ◆ sun/partial shade	
Propagation ◆ seed	

The native foxglove is very widely distributed throughout the moister parts of Britain. It prefers partial shade, though it is quite often found in the open, and quickly colonises cleared woodlands. The normal colour varies from pinky-rose to purple and although a number of other shades have been developed in cultivated forms, these seem to lack the charm of the native.

Foxglove

Although truly a biennial with a life cycle of two years, it sets seed in profusion and foxgloves can establish themselves very easily. Ideally it should be placed in the moister part of the garden, but the foxglove will succeed in sun provided the soil remains moist. It likes heavy clay, provided that it is well-drained and acid. The foxglove is a superb plant to grow in stately clumps up to 1.5m (5ft) tall to hide a fence or give colour under trees.

Digitalin, the poisonous drug extracted from foxglove, has been used widely in the treatment of heart disease.

A related member of the same botanical family is the monkeyflower (*Mimulus guttatus*). This is a very much shorter plant and in the garden will grow to no more than 30cm (12in). The flowers are bright yellow with bright red spots at the throat, rather similar in shape to the foxglove and it grows in similar moist situations but prefers light shade to full sun. Closely related are the cultivated varieties of mimulus which are very colourful and like all monkeyflowers, succeed well on the shady side of a pond.

◆ FRITILLARY ◆

Fritillaria meleagris

Flowering season ◆ April to May	
Soil ◆ moist	
Acidity ◆ neutral/alkaline	
Situation ◆ sun, ponds and marsh	
Propagation ◆ seed/division	

Also commonly known as 'snake's-head', this lovely bulbous plant is possibly not a true native, though it was once quite common in water meadows and other moist grassland. Nowadays fritillary is extremely rare in the wild and virtually confined to nature reserves. It has a range of other common names, including 'guinea-fowl-flower', 'sullen-lady', 'drooping-tulip', 'turkey-eggs', 'widow's-veil' and 'toads'-heads'. All refer either to the shape or colour of the very distinctive flowerheads.

Fritillary has also been grown widely as a garden plant for several centuries and this is where it mainly survives today. The bulbs grow best naturalised in damp grassland on fairly heavy soil,

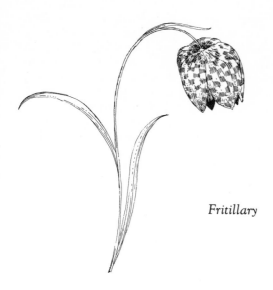

Fritillary

This native perennial is the most striking member of the speedwell family and is very widely distributed in open woodlands and on grassy banks. The mid-blue flowers with a white eye emerge very early and carry on through the spring and summer, though they close at night and in bad weather. The name 'germander' originally meant oak-like and refers to the shape of the leaves. Other common country names are 'blue-eyes', 'bird's-eye' and 'cat's-eye'.

In the garden, germander speedwell is too vigorous for the open border but it is a good inhabitant of a wild garden or any area where it can be left to ramble unchecked, such as a hedge bottom. It grows to a height of about 40cm (16in) and will make a good weed-smothering ground cover. Germander speedwell is also a good plant to grow in rough grass, which should not be cut too short and is clipped sparingly whilst the speedwell is flowering.

Of the other fourteen or so speedwells growing in the wild, most native but some naturalised, the annual, common field-speedwell (*V. persica*) is a widespread agricultural weed and also spreads in lawns, where it forms a good contrast to the early-flowering daisy. Ivy-leaved speedwell (*V. hederifolia*) is also an annual but can be a useful creeping plant to grow over a stone or brick wall for the sake of the leaf cover. The flowers are lilac or white but quite tiny and insignificant. Wood speedwell (*V. montana*) is a perennial which grows in moist woodland with a larger leaf and lilac flower and can be useful for a very shady garden.

though this needs to be well-drained as they will not tolerate marshy conditions. Fritillary tolerates moist light shade under trees and will also succeed in good soil as a front-of-border and rockery plant. Once well established it will self-seed happily but off-sets from the bulbs can be lifted and re-planted when the foliage has died down.

The plants grow to about 45cm (18in) and each carries one or two drooping and nodding bell-like flowers. Most flowers are purple with creamy-white cross-hatchings, but white with green markings is not unusual and there are cross-bred intermediate forms. The seedheads are also beautiful and can be used for winter decoration after being dried and varnished. The seed can be saved for sowing – though seedlings take several years to flower.

◆ GERMANDER ◆
SPEEDWELL
Veronica chamaedrys

Flowering season ◆ **March to July**	
Soil ◆ **normal border/poor dry**	
Acidity ◆ **acid/alkaline**	
Situation ◆ **sun/partial shade, meadow**	
Propagation ◆ **seed/division**	

Germander speedwell

Globeflower

◆ GLOBEFLOWER ◆

Trollius europaeus

Flowering season ◆ June to August	
Soil ◆ moist	
Acidity ◆ neutral/acid	
Situation ◆ sun/partial shade	
Propagation ◆ seed/division	

This showy native perennial relative of the butter-cups is found in wet woodlands, grassland and scrub in the wilds of Scotland, northern England and Wales. It has the divided leaves of the rest of the family but with much more globular and larger lemon-yellow flowers standing well clear of the foliage. Over-picking may have helped it become much harder to find.

The globeflower is not grown so widely in gardens as the cultivated hybrid trollius, which have been developed with larger flowers and colours ranging from pale lemon to deep orange, but it remains a delightful plant. The best situation is in a marsh or beside a pond but it will also grow in a moist border provided the soil is not chalky. In good soil the flowers reach about 60cm (2ft) tall and are attractive to bees and other small pollinating insects. It needs planting in a clump to be seen at its best.

The marsh-marigold or king-cup (*Caltha palustris*) is closely related to globeflower and also grows in wet places. It flowers earlier, with glossy green leaves and golden single blooms that always seem to look best reflected in water. It can be grown right at the pond edge, where it will stand being flooded with several inches of water, or in wet borders and wild gardens mixed with other moisture loving flowers such as meadowsweet, yellow iris and purple-loosestrife. Nurserymen have developed both single and double white forms of the king-cup.

GREATER ◆ KNAPWEED ◆

Centaurea scabiosa

Flowering season ◆ June to September	
Soil ◆ normal border	
Acidity ◆ neutral/alkaline	
Situation ◆ sun, meadow	
Propagation ◆ seed/division	

This native perennial relative of the cornflower is found growing mainly in the east and south-east of England on chalky grassland, in hedgerows and on roadsides. The purple-crimson flowers make the greater knapweed a more conspicuous plant than the common, black or lesser knapweed (*C. nigra*), which is shorter and has a smaller flower.

In the garden the greater knapweed deserves to be a much better-known plant. It likes a position in full sun and can be grown either in the open border or as a constituent of a flowering meadow. In good soil it will grow up to 90cm (3ft) tall but less in poorer soil or in grass. The leaves are also very attractive, being deeply divided and often over 30cm (12in) long. Both the flowers and unopened buds are good for cutting and can be dried. The seedheads are formed by over-lapping bracts and are most attractive. The unopened buds of common knapweed are also very distinctive and provide the common name of 'hardheads'.

Both the greater and common knapweeds are among the best wild flowers for feeding butterflies. They are also attractive to bees while seed-eating birds like the goldfinch will plunder the seeds.

The flowers of greater knapweed were eaten in the past for digestive disorders and an ointment made from the plant for treating wounds. Petals from hardheads have been recommended as an addition to salads.

Greater knapweed

GREATER
◆ STITCHWORT ◆

Stellaria holostea

Flowering season ◆ **April to June**	
Soil ◆ **normal border**	
Acidity ◆ **acid/neutral**	
Situation ◆ **sun/partial shade**	
Propagation ◆ **seed**	

This is a widespread perennial flower of woods, hedgerows and roadsides throughout much of Britain. The white star-like flowers are a feature of the countryside in spring and have a number of other names including 'adders'-meat' and 'brandy-snap'. Other close relatives are the lesser stitchwort, slightly taller and usually growing on lighter soil, marsh stitchwort which grows in wet spots, and wood stitchwort which flowers rather later. The name of stitchwort seems to refer to its one-time use against stitches and other pains in the side.

In the garden greater stitchwort grows to about 60cm (2ft) tall in good soil and makes an excellent ground cover either in a mixed border or in a naturalised wild garden. It is also a useful plant for grassy banks or in damp semi-shade under tall trees, where the weak stems ramble over other low-growing plants. This is not a good flower for picking as the weak stems seem to break as soon as they are touched.

The humble close cousin of the stitchworts is chickweed (*S. media*). Despite not generally being regarded as a gardener's friend, this is a plant which has been widely used in the past, both cooked as a vegetable, fresh as a winter salad and to treat medical problems as diverse as sore eyes, inflammation of the skin, boils and coughs, and as a gentle laxative. It was also fed to fowls, hence the name, and both leaves and seeds are very attractive to a number of birds.

Greater stitchwort

Great mullein

GREAT
◆ MULLEIN ◆
Verbascum thapsus

Flowering season ◆	June to July
Soil ◆	normal border
Acidity ◆	neutral/acid/alkaline
Situation ◆	sun
Propagation ◆	seed

Also known as 'Aaron's-rod', the great mullein is a tall, stately, native biennial fairly common on sunny banks and waste places. The closely related dark mullein (*Verbascum nigrum*) is also a biennial but not so tall and is far less common in the wild. It will also tolerate slightly more shade and a chalky soil and is often found under hedges and along the roadside.

In good garden soil the great mullein grows up to 2.15m (7ft) tall and can be seen at its best either at the back of a border, or dotted between low and medium growing shrubs. Grown in clumps, the single spike densely covered with bright yellow flowers, together with the silvery foliage give a striking effect to a wild garden. In an exposed position the stems will need support in windy weather.

The dark mullein grows to about 1.2m (4ft) in the garden and produces a larger number of flowering spikes on each plant. It has darker green leaves than the great mullein and the yellow blooms have purple centres. It is most effective

grown in clumps rather than as a single plant.

Being biennial, both mulleins produce a rosette of leaves in the first year followed by flowers in the second. Initially they will need sowing for two years running to make sure of a continuity of flowers and self-set seedlings. Both are attractive to bees and the great mullein is home to the handsome mullein moth. Great mullein has been used for herbal tobacco.

Green hellebore

GREEN
◆ HELLEBORE ◆
Helleborus viridis

Flowering season ◆	March to May
Soil ◆	normal border/moist
Acidity ◆	alkaline
Situation ◆	partial shade/shade
Propagation ◆	seed/division

This and the related stinking hellebore (*H. foetidus*) are rather rare native perennials found in chalky woodlands scattered throughout England and Wales. They are both close relatives of the well-loved Christmas-rose, a native of central and southern Europe, and the later-flowering Lenten-rose, which came originally from Greece and Asia Minor.

The green hellebore establishes well in quite heavy shade, though it will also grow in some sunshine. It likes good soil, where it will grow up to 45cm (18in), but it tolerates poor drainage and quite wet conditions. Green hellebore is best grown in a quiet spot in the garden where it can remain undisturbed and the large, green flowers may be seen at their best against a dark background. Somewhat unusually for a herbaceous plant, the foliage dies down in summer but often appears again by January.

Stinking hellebore, also known as 'oxheal', grows to about 60cm (2ft) and is a more handsome garden plant than green hellebore and more-or-less evergreen throughout the year. It also flowers earlier and the blooms are smaller but carried in larger bunches, and with the edges of the petals marked strongly with purple. These last for a long time and attract early-flying insects.

Both hellebores are poisonous but not especially attractive to children. The leaves dry well for winter flower decoration and fresh stinking hellebore is attractive in a spring arrangement with bulbs and other flowers.

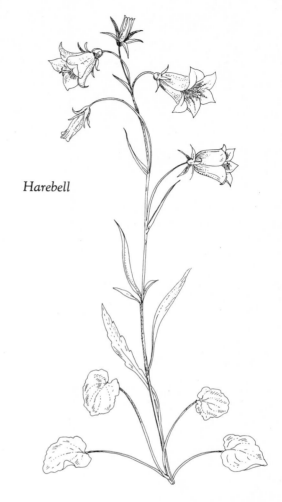

Harebell

· HAREBELL ·

Campanula rotundifolia

Flowering season ◆ July to September	
Soil ◆ normal border/poor and dry	
Acidity ◆ alkaline/acid	
Situation ◆ sun/partial shade, meadow	
Propagation ◆ seed, stratification advised/cuttings	

This native perennial is the bluebell of Scotland, but the harebell and the English bluebell really are in quite different families. Although at one time very common on southern grassy chalk downlands, the harebell is very tolerant of soil and site and can be found in many other types of places such as wastelands, sand dunes, roadsides and even peat bogs throughout much of Britain. Its other local names of 'witchbell' and 'witches' thimble' may have come from a long-held popular association between hares and witchcraft.

Harebell is one of the smaller native members of the quite large bellflower family, of which there are also a number of good cultivated and imported forms. In the wild the graceful, nodding flowers can vary from pale to darker blue and there is also a rather rare white form. The main leaves on the stem are sparse and insignificant, but those at the base are round like many other campanulas and gave the name to the species.

A mini-meadow makes an ideal site for harebells but it will need managing rather like a sheep-grazed downland if they are to establish and be seen at their best. In good soil they will grow to a height of about 40cm (16in) so are ideal plants for the front of a border or in the taller parts of the rock garden, where they form a contrast to lower-growing alpine bellflower species. They are also good plants for flowering later in the summer in pots, boxes and tubs and will also establish in the crevices of paths and walls, though growing much lower.

◆ HONEYSUCKLE ◆

Lonicera periclymenum

Flowering season ◆ June to September	
Soil ◆ normal border	
Acidity ◆ acid/alkaline	
Situation ◆ sun/partial shade	
Propagation ◆ cuttings	

The native wild honeysuckle or woodbine is a very common wild flower of woods, hedges and scrubland throughout Britain, where it roots in the shady cool and twines out into the sun, always in a clockwise direction. It has creamy-white and pink or crimson buds and is generally stronger scented than other deciduous or semi-evergreen garden hybrids and other imported honeysuckle species listed by nurserymen. Some of these can also be found in the wild as garden escapes.

In the garden wild honeysuckle grows to about 1.8m (6ft) and being self-training, is very useful for covering an unsightly fence or wall. It will also ramble over a garden arch or pergola or climb through an old apple or pear tree. If the annual growth is kept pruned, it even makes a free-standing shrub. It will grow in poor soil in really heavy shade but needs to flower in the sun to be seen at its best. In addition to the masses of sweet-smelling flowers, honeysuckle produces bright red berries in the autumn which, though poisonous to humans, attract some birds.

Producing plenty of nectar, honeysuckle attracts a wide range of insects, especially long-tongued moths who fly at night when the scent is strongest, and some butterflies which also feed on the leaves. Humbles are the only bees able to obtain nectar and pollen from the blossoms, which, like runner beans, they tackle by biting through the base of the flowering tubes. Children also used to pick the blooms and suck out the nectar.

Honeysuckle

◆ JACOB'S-LADDER ◆

Polemonium caeruleum

Flowering season ◆ May to July	
Soil ◆ normal border	
Acidity ◆ neutral/alkaline	
Situation ◆ sun/partial shade	
Propagation ◆ seed/division	

Part of the name comes from the paired leaflets carried on rather fern-like bright green leaves, which have something of the appearance of a step-ladder. The reference to Jacob is almost certainly biblical.

This is a long-time favourite of cottage gardens and is now regarded as a cultivated plant. Although a native, Jacob's-ladder is now quite rare and original wild populations are found only in the north of England. Plants growing in the wild in other areas are garden escapes. Its natural home is in fertile, chalky and often moist soils growing in full sun or light shade. The 2½cm (1in) wide flowers are carried in multi-clusters and white when in

Jacob's-ladder

bud, but come out cobalt-blue with conspicuous, bright yellow anthers. A white form has also been cultivated.

Jacob's-ladder has only a single native species but it is related to the cultivated garden phlox and prefers similar garden conditions. In good soil it grows to about 60cm (2ft) and is best sited as a showy plant for the middle of a mixed border, rather than in a wild garden. It likes heavy, fertile soils which hold moisture and will appreciate mulching in dry weather. It sets seed readily and although by no means aggressive, if allowed to seed, a single plant will grow into a clump quite quickly.

The individual flowers can be dried for flower pictures and cards, but make sure that the yellow anthers are retained.

◆ LADY'S BEDSTRAW ◆

Galium verum

Flowering season ◆ **June to August**	
Soil ◆ **normal border/poor and dry**	
Acidity ◆ **acid/alkaline**	
Situation ◆ **sun, meadow**	
Propagation ◆ **seed/division**	

Known in medieval times as Our Lady's bedstraw because of the legend that it formed part of the bedding in the stable at Bethlehem. This is a very common native, low-growing perennial wild flower found widely by the roadside, on sandy heaths and as a weed of lawns in light soil. The related hedge bedstraw (*G. mollugo*) is a taller plant and not so colourful but can also make a useful plant in the garden. Another close relative is cleavers (*G. aparine*), or 'sweethearts', a widespread agricultural weed which has no garden value but had both culinary and medical uses in the past.

The best place in the garden for lady's bedstraw is a flowering meadow, left uncut while it flowers in summer. There it will grow to about 45cm (18in), producing masses of greenish-yellow flowers and spreading very quickly through the grass. It also makes a good border plant, where the flowers with the contrasting whorls of delicate, dark green leaves are seen at their best on a plant growing to about 90cm (3ft). It is a good plant for cutting, lasting well in water, and the dried seed-heads are useful for winter flower arrangement.

In addition to the straw being used to fill mattresses, lady's bedstraw was used widely to curdle milk for cheese-making, with the flowers also giving a rich colour to the cheese. This gave the alternative names of 'cheese-rennet' and 'cud-wort'. Medically it was used as a diuretic and a footbath, while the roots of hedge bedstraw made a bright red dye.

Lady's bedstraw

This meadow (*left*) shows common poppy, corncockle and cornflowers. Other flourishing meadow flowers include ragged-robin with meadow buttercup (*above right*) and smooth hawk's-beard with oxeye daisy (*below right*).

Lady's-mantle

◆ LADY'S-MANTLE ◆

Alchemilla vulgaris

Flowering season ◆ June to September	
Soil ◆ normal border/moist	
Acidity ◆ acid/alkaline	
Situation ◆ sun/partial shade	
Propagation ◆ seed/division	

There are a number of species of this delightfully-named perennial native wild flower but it can take a botanist to tell them apart. It is also very similar to the cultivated alchemilla, which is not a native and really not a much better garden plant. In the wild the most common lady's-mantle grows in moist meadows and open woodlands but there are other types which prefer drier conditions and an alpine species which thrives on rocky, mountain ledges.

In the garden this species of lady's-mantle is extremely useful as a low-growing plant with abundant large leaves, giving the alternative name of 'lion's-foot', which smother weeds for much of the year. It grows to about 45cm (18in), less in poor soil, and is equally effective for ground-cover in a mixed border or in a wild garden.

The small, greeny-yellow flowers, which are actually the calyx and not true petals, are carried in large bunches which look attractive even when many of the blossoms are over. The young foliage, pale green on top and grey underneath, is particularly attractive in spring. In good soil lady's-

mantle spreads quite rapidly and if other plants are not to be smothered, may need thinning out every year.

Lady's-mantle is invaluable for winter arrangements, but it must be picked before the flowers turn brown and stood in buckets for thorough drying.

LARGE-FLOWERED ◆ EVENING-PRIMROSE ◆

Oenothera erythrosepala

Flowering season ◆ June to September	
Soil ◆ normal border	
Acidity ◆ neutral/alkaline	
Situation ◆ sun	
Propagation ◆ seed	

None of the evening-primroses are true natives and come from either North or South America, but since being introduced have spread quite

Large-flowered evening-primrose

rapidly to waste places, roadsides, sand dunes and railway embankments and cuttings (a common highway for the spread of a number of introduced plants). They are not related in any way to the true British primrose but might have been misnamed due to their yellow flowers.

In the garden the large, yellow-flowered evening-primrose grows to over 90cm (3ft), more in fertile, well-drained soil. It has large leaves as well as flowers, which come out on summer evenings as the sun gets lower in the sky and only last for a single day. As it can be blown over by strong winds, it grows best as a clump in a mixed border where there are other plants to support and protect it. Although biennial, it self-seeds easily and often flowers in the first year.

Of the other naturalised species, fragrant evening-primrose (*O. stricta*) is not such a striking plant as it has smaller, thinner leaves and not such large or showy blossoms. However, the beautiful scent can fill the garden on a still, summer evening. It is not so tall but grows more erect and will support itself better in exposed conditions. It also tolerates some shade.

Although not widely used medically in the past, extracts of evening-primrose now show promise in treating heart disease and multiple sclerosis.

Lesser celandine

LESSER
◆ CELANDINE ◆

Ranunculus ficaria

Flowering season ◆ **March to May**	
Soil ◆ **normal border/moist**	
Acidity ◆ **neutral**	
Situation ◆ **partial shade/shade**	
Propagation ◆ **seed/division**	

One of the earliest spring flowers, this member of the buttercup family is well worth a place in any garden. It is not related to the greater celandine (*Chelidonium majus*), which is a much bigger plant and from an entirely different botanical family.

Lesser celandine is a common native perennial flowering in wet ditches and woodlands, sometimes on sites in heavy shade for the rest of the year. The first sign of spring in the countryside is often the emergence of the glossy green celandine leaves, followed a few days later by the shining gold eight or more petalled flowers, with their ring of deep yellow stamens. The flowers are borne on stems about 20cm (8in) long. Soon after flowering ceases the leaves die down, the plant rests in the soil as a small tuber which can then withstand quite dry conditions.

A good place in the garden to grow lesser celandine is at the base of a deciduous tree, where it will mix well with spring flowering bulbs, violets and the wood anemone. It also brightens up the base of hedges and other dark areas. It will spread too vigorously for most flower borders because it forms masses of little tubers which, once established, are difficult to eradicate. Lifting, splitting and re-planting some of these tubers soon after the leaves have died down is a good way to propagate it.

'Pilewort' is a no-nonsense country name showing a one-time medical use for lesser celandine. More attractive is the alternative 'golden guineas'.

◆ LILY-OF-THE-VALLEY ◆

Convallaria majalis

Flowering season ◆ **May to June**	
Soil ◆ **normal border**	
Acidity ◆ **neutral/acid**	
Situation ◆ **partial shade/shade**	
Propagation ◆ **division**	

This is such a widespread garden plant that it can come as a surprise to learn that it is a native member of the lily family. In the wild it grows in dry woodlands, mainly in England and Wales, but is now rare and scattered. Drifts in old wooded parkland are probably garden escapes. Other popular names include 'Mary's-tears', 'fairy-bells' and 'May-lily'.

One reason that lily-of-the-valley sometimes fails in gardens is that it is planted frequently in dry soil in full sun. It really needs quite a lot of shade, especially in the summer, and is one of the few plants which will succeed with no direct sunlight at all. This makes it very useful for any shady, dark but well-drained corner with peat or leaf mould worked into the soil, where it spreads by underground rhizomes to form large clumps carrying an abundance of fragrant, white flowers. The broad leaves stay green all summer and provide good ground cover before turning golden-yellow in autumn. It grows to about 30cm (12in).

Lily-of-the-valley

Lily-of-the-valley was once widely forced in greenhouses to give cut flowers in winter and it also makes a good flowering house plant. Split into small clumps in October for growing indoors in pots in gentle heat, but if cutting the flowers for decoration, leave as many leaves as possible on each clump. It can also be put into a tub or box to stand on a shaded patio. Although poisonous, an extract made from lily-of-the-valley is still used as an alternative to digitalin to help regulate the heart.

◆ MALE-FERN ◆

Dryopteris filix-mas

Flowering season ◆ **none**	
Soil ◆ **normal border**	
Acidity ◆ **acid/alkaline**	
Situation ◆ **sun/partial shade**	
Propagation ◆ **division**	

This is probably one of the most widespread of our native ferns and grows in large numbers in a range of situations, from open heathland to the banks of streams and country lanes. It can be mistaken for bracken, and is known as fern-bracken in Cumberland, but instead of creeping roots has a central rootstock growing hard and woody with age.

Another local name for the male-fern is 'dead-man's hands', from the supposed resemblance of the unrolling fronds in spring to a clenched fist. It makes a very handsome garden plant and is one of the most tolerant of soil and situation. The male fern is probably best seen against a sunny wall and in good soil can grow up to 1.2m (4ft). It stands dry conditions.

Hart's tongue (*Phyllitis scolopendrium*) is a totally different looking fern with strap-shaped leaves and to the uninitiated might even appear to be some form of dock. These leaves vary tremendously from about 5 cm (2in) long when grown out of a wall to up to 90cm (3ft) when growing in a ditch or other wet conditions. In addition to needing moisture to grow well, this is a plant for heavy shade, where it is semi-evergreen and gives colour all winter.

Maidenhair (*Adiantum capillus-veneris*) is another native fern, now very rare in the wild but

Male-fern

popular as an indoor foliage plant. Its natural home is in the rocks and crannies of the south-west of England; elsewhere as a garden plant it needs protection at the base of a wall, covering against frost in a hard winter and plenty of moisture.

MARSH
·WOUNDWORT·

Stachys palustris

Flowering season ◆ **July to September**	
Soil ◆ **moist**	
Acidity ◆ **neutral/acid**	
Situation ◆ **partial shade/shade, ponds and marsh**	
Propagation ◆ **seed/division**	

This native perennial grows in the wild by ponds and streams and in fens and marshes. Although not one of the most striking of wild flowers, the delicate purple-pink flowers and spear-shaped leaves on square stems make it quite attractive. With the closely related hedge woundwort (*S. sylvatica*), the antiseptic qualities of the leaves were used widely in the past for the treatment of cuts and bruises – hence the name.

Marsh woundwort is most useful in the garden by the shady side of a pond or in wet soil, where the leaves and flowers form a useful background for smaller plants. It grows to about 75cm (30in) and is not suitable for a mixed border unless the soil stays very moist throughout the summer.

Hedge woundwort is also perennial and makes a taller plant, with the flowering stems growing to 1.05m (3ft 6in). In the wild this species grows in drier soil in woods, hedges and other shady places. In the garden it will tolerate some sun but is another useful plant for growing in quite dense shade, where it flowers rather earlier in the year than marsh woundwort. The flowers are attractive to bees and a fairly close relative is the garden stachys or 'lamb's tongues'.

In addition to treating wounds, both the woundworts have been used in the past as a gargle against inflammation of the throat and drunk as a tea against digestive disorders and as a general tonic.

Marsh woundwort

◆ MEADOW CLARY ◆

Salvia pratensis

Flowering season ◆ **June to July**	
Soil ◆ **normal border**	
Acidity ◆ **neutral/alkaline**	
Situation ◆ **sun**	
Propagation ◆ **seed/division**	

This is a somewhat rare native member of the mint and sage family and grows on chalky grassland in southern England. It has beautiful blue flowers carried on long spikes and large, fleshy leaves at the base but very few on the stems. More common is the wild clary (*S. horminoides*) found on roadsides, dry grassland and waste places throughout southern England. It is a much less decorative plant but can be useful for growing in rough grassland.

Meadow clary has been grown in cottage gardens for many years and is regarded as a valuable perennial border plant. There are also cultivated forms varying from deeper blue to pink and white. Grown in clumps in a well-drained, sunny border it grows to about 75cm (30in) and gives a very striking display. Like the sages, the large wrinkled and toothed leaves are aromatic when crushed.

Sometimes confused with meadow clary is clary-sage (*S. sclarea*) but although in the same family, this is a much taller biennial from southern

Europe with coloured bracts invaluable for flower arrangement.

Another useful member of this family is white horehound (*Marrubium vulgare*), fairly common on roadsides throughout England and Wales and rather similar in shape to cat-mint. Growing to about 45cm (18in) it makes a useful white-flowering plant for a dry border and is very attractive to bees. Tea made from it was once used as a standard country remedy against coughs and colds.

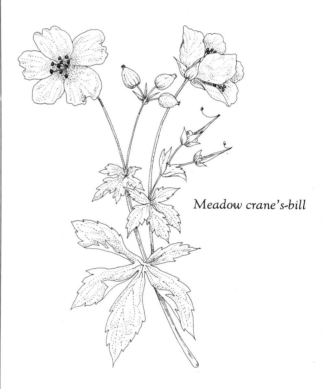

Meadow crane's-bill

Meadow clary

MEADOW ◆ CRANE'S-BILL ◆

Geranium pratense

Flowering season ◆ **May to September**	
Soil ◆ **normal border**	
Acidity ◆ **neutral/alkaline**	
Situation ◆ **sun**	
Propagation ◆ **seed, scarification advised/division**	

There are some 16 native true geraniums or crane's-bills (see page 70 for some of the others) and also a number of very good cultivated garden varieties. All grow well on limy soils. They are named after a supposed resemblance between the beak and head of crane and their elongated seedhead, rather than the flower.

Meadow crane's-bill is the most common species found in the wild and also one of the most showy in flower. It grows in limestone and other chalky areas on roadsides and banks, mainly in the south of Britain. The large, purple-blue blossoms are carried in clusters and some flowers can be found in every month of summer.

On good soil meadow crane's-bill will spread vigorously and grow to about 75cm (30in) in height. It makes a free-flowering border plant but can be invasive, especially if left to seed, so is often best placed in a wild garden where it can be better controlled. It also grows well in rough grass. In addition to the masses of flowers, it also has handsome, deeply divided bright green foliage all summer turning a russet colour in autumn.

Wood crane's-bill (*G. sylvaticum*) grows to a similar height with pinker flowers and is a good alternative to grow in a moist, shady site and on more acid soil. Apart from parts of Scotland it is quite rare in the wild so is well worth preserving in gardens.

MEADOW
◆ SAXIFRAGE ◆

Saxifraga granulata

Flowering season ◆ April to June	
Soil ◆ normal border	
Acidity ◆ neutral/alkaline	
Situation ◆ sun/partial shade, meadow	
Propagation ◆ seed/cutting	

This is a native lowland species of a large family widely spread through many of the mountainous regions of the world and very widely grown in gardens. Meadow saxifrage grows in grassland and is fairly scattered throughout most of England and parts of Scotland but rare in Wales. It prefers to live undisturbed and possibly for this reason is

Meadow saxifrage

quite often found in the grass of country churchyards.

In good soil, the pure white flowers carried on long stems grow up to about 45cm (18in). The foliage is green and rounded and quite large for a saxifrage. It can be grown in a flower border but as most of the leaves die down soon after flowering, it is normally better used in a flowering meadow. Although suitable for a rockery, there are some better species.

One of these is the purple saxifrage (*S. oppositifolia*), which lives in the wild mainly on mountains in northern Scotland. It only grows to about 15cm (6in), likes crevices in damp rocks and stony ground and flowers from March to May and sometimes again in July and August. The flowers are carried on rather sprawling stems and vary from pink to violet-purple and there are some bright crimson cultivated forms.

The very dwarf golden-saxifrage (*Chrysosplenium oppositifolium*) comes from wet places throughout Britain and likes an acid soil. The flowers are greeny-yellow but the foliage is an attractive, fleshy bright gold and has been eaten as a vegetable.

◆ MEADOWSWEET ◆

Filipendula ulmaria

Flowering season ◆ **June to August**	
Soil ◆ **moist**	
Acidity ◆ **neutral/alkaline**	
Situation ◆ **sun/partial shade, ponds and marshes**	
Propagation ◆ **seed/division**	

This handsome native perennial plant is common throughout Britain in wet meadows, marshes, ditches and other wet places. Also known as 'queen-of-the-meadow', meadowsweet is a plant of great antiquity. It has recently been identified as an ingredient of the remnants of a 4,000 year-old neolithic drink found in the Hebrides.

Meadowsweet makes a valuable plant for pond edges, mini-marshes and even moist borders. In good soil and without competition it can grow to over 90cm (3ft), with feathery heads of creamy-white scented blossoms and elm-like leaves green on top and grey underneath. The cultivated shrubby spireas and the stately white aruncus are closely related.

Meadowsweet

The fragrance of meadowsweet made it a popular flower for strewing in medieval houses and churches and for this it was a favourite of Elizabeth I. It was also used to flavour mead and other drinks, hence the original name of 'mead-sweet' or 'meadwort', and also for curing fevers and digestive disorders.

Dropwort (*F. vulgaris*) is a very close relative which grows on drier soils and in sunnier sites. It is rather shorter than meadowsweet with rose-coloured buds opening to rather similar white, fluffy flowers carried on smaller heads. The fern-like foliage and dainty appearance makes this a very good plant for a mixed, dry border and it deserves being better known.

◆ MUSK MALLOW ◆

Malva moschata

Flowering season ◆ **June to August**	
Soil ◆ **normal border**	
Acidity ◆ **neutral/alkaline**	
Situation ◆ **sun/partial shade**	
Propagation ◆ **seed/cuttings**	

This is the prettiest of all the native species of the mallow family. A perennial plant, it grows in the wild in well-drained meadows, on grassy banks and along the roadside. It is common throughout southern Britain but much rarer elsewhere, except where it has escaped from cultivation. The flowers are usually a clear rose-pink with slightly darker spots and veining, but there is also a white form which has been selected out as a garden variety.

On good garden soil on a well-drained site musk mallow grows to about 45cm (18in), while the finely divided leaves on the flower stems provide another attraction and are good for floral arrangement. It makes a good plant for a mixed border but also contrasts well with other species in a wild garden. Both the flowers and leaves are scented and attractive to bees for nectar and pollen. Hollyhocks, hibiscus and annual lavatera are three important mallows widely grown in gardens.

Common mallows (*M. sylvestris*) is a larger plant, more widespread in the wild, with rose-purple flowers and much fleshier leaves. It is not such a

Musk mallow

good garden plant but can be useful for growing against a hedge or unsightly wall. Marsh-mallow (*Althaea officinalis*) lives in salt marshes and ditches near the sea but is rather rare. An extract from the roots gave the name to the rather sticky sweet.

A tea made from the common mallow was drunk against coughs and bronchitis and the round fruits eaten as a vegetable.

· MUSK THISTLE ·

Carduus nutans

Flowering season ◆ May to August
Soil ◆ normal border
Acidity ◆ neutral/alkaline
Situation ◆ sun
Propagation ◆ seed

Not all thistles are pernicious weeds and there are several species worth growing in a garden. One is musk thistle, a very handsome native plant growing in meadows, hedgerows, roadsides and waste places. The large, purple-reddish flowers are carried on spiky stems with long, strap-shaped spiny leaves. Other names are nodding thistle, from the way the heads sway in the wind, and musk thistle from the faintly scented flowers. It grows up to about 90cm (3ft) and makes a good specimen plant for the rear of a mixed border or in a wild garden. It is biennial but seeds set easily and once planted soon becomes established.

Cotton thistle (*Onopordon acanthium*) is also biennial and probably not a true native, though it now grows widely in waste places in the east of England. It is a tall, stately plant growing up to 3m (10ft) in good garden soil, with large purply-coloured flowers. The main feature is the silver-white covering of cobweb-like hairs on the stems and foliage, which makes cotton thistle a notable feature for any border, though it needs a largish garden to be seen at its best. It seeds very readily and can be invasive unless the seedlings are thinned.

Both these thistles, and others, are attractive to butterflies. Useful dwarf species are the autumn-flowering carline thistle (*Carlina vulgaris*), melancholy thistle (*C. helenoides*), named after the drooping heads, and meadow thistle (*C. dissectum*) for wet soils.

Musk thistle

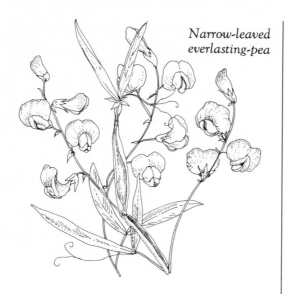

*Narrow-leaved
everlasting-pea*

NARROW-LEAVED
·EVERLASTING-PEA·

Lathyrus sylvestris

Flowering season ◆ **June to August**	
Soil ◆ **normal border**	
Acidity ◆ **neutral/alkaline**	
Situation ◆ **sun/partial shade**	
Propagation ◆ **seed, scarification advised/division**	

This perennial native is now quite rare in the wild and a relative of the cultivated garden sweet peas, which originated in southern Europe and since bred to produce a range of scented colours. The everlasting-sweet-pea grown in gardens is usually another species properly called the broad-leaved everlasting-pea (*L. latifolius*), an introduction from Europe sometimes seen in the wild when it has escaped from cultivation. The main difference is the width of the leaves and stipules, which are the little leaflets between leaf and stem.

The flowers of the narrow-leaved everlasting-pea are a single colour of creamy-yellow flushed with deep pink or crimson; those of the broad-leaved type red and purple. Both are smaller than the best sweet-peas but are carried in profusion though, unfortunately, have no scent. The plants of each produce a number of basal stems and climb by tendrils, which cling to any support and like to flower in either sun or light shade.

The height of both is about 1.5m (5ft) in good soil and they are very useful plants to ramble over an old wall or fence, or even the lower branches of an old apple tree or shrub. They can also be trained over tall pea sticks at the back of a flowering border.

Like sweet-peas, the everlastings keep blooming longer if dead-headed and they also make good cut flowers, though without the scent and range of colours of their cultivated cousins.

·OXEYE DAISY·

Leucanthemum vulgare

Flowering season ◆ **May to August**	
Soil ◆ **normal border**	
Acidity ◆ **acid/alkaline**	
Situation ◆ **sun, meadow**	
Propagation ◆ **seed/division**	

Oxeye daisy

In the wild this most popular perennial native wild flower once lived in many old meadows but nowadays is found mostly on roadside grassy banks and verges. It was also commonly grown in cottage gardens and given several other names such as 'moon daisy', 'dog daisy' and 'marguerite'. Cultivated double white shasta daisies like the well-known Esther Read and Wirral pride are fairly close relatives, though not native to this country.

In the garden the oxeye daisy can be treated as a border plant and if planted in good soil it will make quite large clumps, carrying many single white flowers and growing up to about 60cm (2ft) tall. Unless kept under control it can be invasive and, like the shasta daisies, might need digging up and splitting every two or three years.

Often a better place to grow the oxeye daisy is in grass, either sown in a meadow mixture or planted out in grassy corners. It looks especially effective in early summer surrounded by the stems of flowering grasses and is also useful to take over from the naturalised spring-flowering bulbs.

The flowers of oxeye daisy are attractive to bees, butterflies and other insects for their nectar. Conversely, planted around the house it is supposed to deter flies. The plant is said to have been a tonic, and syrup was made from it to treat catarrh and ulcers. The strongly aromatic leaves and roots were used to flavour soups and stews.

◆ PASQUEFLOWER ◆

Pulsatilla vulgaris

Flowering season ◆ April to May	
Soil ◆ normal border	
Acidity ◆ alkaline	
Situation ◆ sun	
Propagation ◆ seed/division	

A rare native perennial in the wild, this is now found on only a few isolated sites growing in the grass of hilly chalk or limestone slopes in east and central England. The name is derived from the time of flowering at Passiontide but it is sometimes also called 'Easter flower' and 'dane's-blood'. It is closely related to all the wild and cultivated anemones.

Pasqueflower

Pasqueflower is a plant of great beauty. This attractiveness, plus changed methods of grassland management, has no doubt helped its disappearance in its natural state but luckily it has long survived in gardens. Although tolerant of a neutral soil, it needs plenty of time to succeed really well. It also needs very good drainage and an ideal site is the sunny side of a rock garden or at the front of an open border. It will grow in thin grass on poor soil but it will not stand much competition.

In good soil the flowers of pasqueflower reach to almost 30cm (12in). They are a true purple, slightly downy, with a mass of golden stamens and hang slightly downwards but wave gently in the wind. A number of coloured shades have also been introduced including white, pink and deep maroon and all are slightly scented. Both stems and the finely divided leaves are also covered in down and large, silky seedheads follow the flowers. If left undisturbed these will set seed and help to increase the stock but being so attractive, they are often picked to add to flower arrangements. A more certain way to propagate the pasqueflower can be to split the clumps in October. The flowers and leaves of the pasqueflower give a green dye which was once used to colour Easter eggs and a tincture from them was a treatment against coughs and bronchitis.

Perennial flax

PERENNIAL
◆ FLAX ◆

Linum perenne subsp. *anglicum*

Flowering season ◆ **June to July**	
Soil ◆ **normal border**	
Acidity ◆ **neutral/alkaline**	
Situation ◆ **sun**	
Propagation ◆ **seed**	

This lovely blue member of the flax family is found on chalky and dry grassland in the east of England, but rarely elsewhere. The smaller and rather insignificant annual purging flax (*L. catharticum*) is much more widespread, also mainly on grassland, and there is another species called pale flax (*L. bienne*) only found in Ireland. The cultivated flax (*L. usitatissimum*), also called linseed and used for the pungent oil, may have been derived originally from pale flax but nowadays is usually known as a separate species.

Although it only flowers for a fairly short season, perennial flax is a useful garden plant as it carries very decorative leaves for the rest of the summer. It grows to about 60cm (2ft), with pale blue flowers with darker markings and a cream

throat carried on slender, arched stems which wave in the wind.

Perennial flax looks best grown in clumps towards the front of a sunny mixed flower border, where it will stand dry conditions, and it makes a good edging for a garden path. The seeds of the pale flax are especially attractive to birds. There are also a number of species of cultivated linum grown in the garden; some are shrubs and others herbaceous plants.

The white-flowered purging or fairy flax (*L. catharticum*) has no great decorative merit but is an interesting plant of under 30cm (12in) to grow in a wild garden or in grass. It was used as a laxative and to treat disorders of the liver.

◆ PRIMROSE ◆

Primula vulgaris

Flowering season ◆ **March to May**	
Soil ◆ **normal border/moist**	
Acidity ◆ **neutral/acid**	
Situation ◆ **partial shade/shade**	
Propagation ◆ **seed, stratification advised/division**	

The primrose is widely spread throughout Britain, usually in moist woodlands, under hedgerows and in other shady places. Although a close relative, it is rarely seen on the same site as the cowslip, which prefers more sunshine, drier soil and open grassland. This is why in the countryside there have always been areas and parishes containing one or the other – seldom both.

The native yellow primrose is an even more attractive garden plant than the cowslip and has suffered considerably in the past from being over-picked, which prevents self-seeding, and from the digging up of plants. The removal of woodlands and hedges, plus the lower standard of management of those that remain, has also led to the loss of many natural habitats.

Thanks to seed raisers there is an increasing supply of natural stocks of primrose seed commercially raised and not taken from the wild. With care, seedlings are not difficult to grow and in a suitable site will establish quite rapidly. The leaves form a rosette up to 12cm (5in) long and slightly

Primrose

This native perennial grows in marshes, swamps, pond edges and other boggy ground throughout much of Britain. The stately spires of purply-red flowers have long been valued for gardens and there are also a number of pink and red cultivated forms. The yellow loosestrife (*Lysimachia vulgaris*) also lives in wet places but has a shorter flowering season, is usually not as tall, is less colourful and is in an entirely different botanical family.

In the garden, purple-loosestrife is best grown in a mini-marsh or on the margins of a pond but it will also make a very striking display in a moist border. In good soil it grows to at least 1.2m (4ft), with flower spikes about 30cm (12in) long and will spread very rapidly if allowed to self-seed. Yellow loosestrife flowers at about the same time so makes a good contrast of flowers and foliage.

The flowers of purple-loosestrife supply plenty of nectar and pollen for bees and butterflies, whilst the caterpillars of the emperor and small elephant hawkmoths feed on the leaves. The dark honey it produces is valued by beekeepers.

Purple-loosestrife has been used fairly widely for treatments including staunching of blood and nosebleeds, the easing of fevers and a number of intestinal complaints. The high tannin content has led to it being used as an alternative to oak bark for tanning leather. Dried yellow loosestrife was burnt in houses to deter flies.

toothed towards the base. The flowers, which are borne on separate stalks up to 20cm (8in) high, have five notched creamy-yellow petals marked with orange-yellow at the centre. Although it will look quite well at the front of a shady, moist border, primroses are at their most natural grown in a semi-wild state at the base of a tree giving shade in summer, or under hedges.

Being such a popular plant, there is a wealth of country lore about the past medical and other uses of the primrose. Like cowslip it makes a good wine and an infusion is said to relieve headaches, migraine and rheumatism.

PURPLE-
◆ LOOSESTRIFE ◆

Lythrum salicaria

Flowering season ◆ **June to August**	
Soil ◆ **moist**	
Acidity ◆ **neutral/alkaline**	
Situation ◆ **sun/partial shade, ponds and marsh**	
Propagation ◆ **seed, cuttings**	

Purple-loosestrife

Ragged-robin

◆ RAGGED-ROBIN ◆

Lychnis flos-cuculi

Flowering season ◆ **May to June**	
Soil ◆ **moist**	
Acidity ◆ **acid/alkaline**	
Situation ◆ **sun/partial shade, ponds and marsh**	
Propagation ◆ **seed/division**	

This is a widespread native perennial which flowers in marshes, fens, wet woods and damp meadows. The term 'ragged' describes the petals, which are rather like a fringed campion but coloured pink instead of red or white. 'Robin' was more likely to have been a medieval jester than the bird and other local names are 'drunkards', 'shaggy jacks' and 'Indian pink', it being a member of the pink and carnation family. Another name in the sixteenth century was the 'crowflower'.

Ragged-robin makes a quite splendid garden flower for wet spots and it will even grow in quite dry borders if kept out of the full sun. The main flowering season ends in June but if the flowering stems are then cut back, it will throw a second flush of bloom until August or even later. It reaches about 60cm (2ft) in height, but can grow taller on good soil. It seeds very profusely, with the seedlings often appearing in the most unlikely places, so needs dead-heading if you do not want to save the seed. Another easy way to propagate it is to divide the clumps in April.

Another good place to see a drift of ragged-robin at its best is in a wet meadow, especially if it goes down to a pond or lake. Ragged-robin is such a vigorous plant that it puts up with fairly close mowing, though the grass should not be cut during the main summer months.

Butterflies are attracted to ragged-robbin, especially the white species.

◆ RAMSONS ◆

Allium ursinum

Flowering season ◆ **April to June**	
Soil ◆ **normal border/moist**	
Acidity ◆ **neutral/acid**	
Situation ◆ **sun/shade**	
Propagation ◆ **seed, stratification advised/division**	

Ramsons

This bulbous plant grows widely in damp woodlands and moist, shady places throughout much of

Britain. Also known as wild garlic, it is the most common native member of the onion family. With a mass of white flowers and a very strong scent when the foliage is crushed, it can truly be said that once smelt never forgotten. It is related to a number of other ornamental onions with coloured flowers and quite decorative foliage, a few native but most imported and very popular in gardens.

Despite the strong scent of the leaves, this is a very useful plant for shaded and woodland areas of a garden, provided they are moist. An ideal situation is open light in early spring when the first flowers appear, followed by leaf shade later as the leaves die down and the bulb rests for the summer. This is a good time to divide clumps of the bulbs if you want to increase your stock.

The somewhat twisted leaves of ramsons rarely grow above 30cm (12in), with the bunches of pure white flowers carried on stems about 15cm (6in) higher. In the wild it often grows in woods with bluebells and as they flower at about the same time, this makes a good combination for the garden.

Other native relatives include chives (*A. schoenoprasum*), also grown as a herb but decorative if allowed to flower and the round-headed leek (*A. sphaerocephalon*), or 'Bristol onion', with a larger head and which is only found in the Avon gorge and in Jersey.

◆ RED CAMPION ◆

Silene dioica

Flowering season ◆ **May to September**	
Soil ◆ **normal border**	
Acidity ◆ **neutral**	
Situation ◆ **sun/partial shade**	
Propagation ◆ **seed/cuttings/division**	

A native biennial or perennial found in the wild over most of Britain in woods, hedges, waste ground and usually shady places. It is a rather more vigorous plant than the closely related white campion (*S. alba*), with which it often hybridises to produce a pink seedling. Unlike white campion, the flowers of which tend to open more in the evening, red campion closes completely at night.

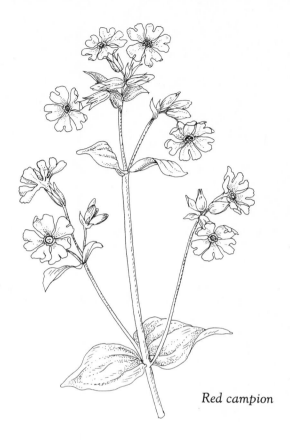

Red campion

The pointed, oval leaves are quite sticky to the touch.

Red campion has long been regarded as a most useful garden flower. In good soil it will grow to at least 55cm (22in), though the plant tends to be rather slender and can be blown over on exposed sites in strong winds. The best way to grow it is in a clump in a mixed border where other plants will give support, or in a fairly dense but open part of a wild garden. Although short-lived it will self-seed itself very easily and a few late flowers will brighten up the garden, often into early winter.

The garden forms and varieties of lychnis are closely related to the campions and grow best in similar slightly shady situations. They are often cut for flower arrangements or drying out but best for this is the native bladder campion (*S. vulgaris*), sometimes known as 'knapbottle' or 'witch's thimble', which is not really a very spectacular garden plant but perfect for winter flower arrangement. The seedheads should be harvested in about August as soon as the flowers are over, dried and varnished.

◆ RED CLOVER ◆

Trifolium pratense

Flowering season ◆ **May to September**	
Soil ◆ **normal border/poor and dry**	
Acidity ◆ **neutral/alkaline**	
Situation ◆ **sun, meadow**	
Propagation ◆ **seed, scarification advised**	

This is one of a very large number of clovers native to this country, some of which have been developed into important agricultural crops. The true wild red clover is a perennial and grows throughout the country in fields, lawns and other grassy places. It is still found in the small amount of old permanent pasture that remains, but in grass leys has been replaced by cultivated varieties, many of which have themselves become naturalised.

The original red clover is smaller, less vigorous and has flowers of a much brighter red. It makes a good constituent of a flowering meadow and provided the soil is not too fertile, will not smother the other species. It thrives in dry conditions but needs free drainage and prefers a chalky soil, where it will grow to about 30cm (12in). A species-rich mixture containing red clover makes good hay for small animals.

Red clover

Another common clover is the wild white (*T. repens*), found on dry waste places and grassy verges throughout the country. The creeping stems of this species can reach 60cm (2ft) in length and although the flower stems reach to 30cm (12in) in the wild, as a weed of lawns it adapts to seed and spread below the height of a cutter. This makes it unpopular with many gardeners, though in a drought clover often provides the only green patches.

Both clovers are attractive to butterflies and white clover is one of the best of all sources of nectar for bees to take for honey.

◆ RED VALERIAN ◆

Centranthus ruber

Flowering season ◆ **May to July**	
Soil ◆ **normal border/poor and dry**	
Acidity ◆ **neutral/alkaline**	
Situation ◆ **sun**	
Propagation ◆ **seed/division**	

Although not a true native, this perennial import from southern Europe is now widely naturalised in southern England and occasionally further north. It grows on dry banks, walls, railway cuttings and in the crevices of cliffs, often quite close to the sea. The native common valerian (*Valeriana officinalis*), although in the same family, is a quite different plant with much larger leaves, a rather insignificant pink flower and few other virtues for the garden.

Red valerian is a very handsome plant and has been justly grown in gardens for a very long time. As a Mediterranean plant it is rather tender and can be damaged on an exposed site in a cold winter. The deep pinky-red flowers are carried in large bunches on stems growing to about 90cm (3ft) in good soil but very much less in walls and on stony, well-drained sites where red valerian is often seen at its best. The stems are sturdy and covered with blue-grey foliage covered with a downy bloom. It spreads rapidly by seed.

There is another related imported type of valerian seen in gardens (var. *rosias*), which is more pink in colour than the red valerian and also has a

Mountain avens (*above*) and alpine cinquefoil (*below*) form the centre point to this rockery.

Red valerian

white form. Both are very attractive to bees and butterflies in mid-summer.

There are no records of any medical use for red valerian, but the young leaves are said to have been eaten in Europe cooked as a vegetable or raw in salads. The native valerian is said to affect the nervous system of cats and to have been used as a bait by rat catchers.

◆ SALAD BURNET ◆

Sanguisorba minor subsp. *minor*

Flowering season ◆ **May to August**	
Soil ◆ **normal border**	
Acidity ◆ **neutral/alkaline**	
Situation ◆ **sun/partial shade**	
Propagation ◆ **seed**	

A perennial native herb, sometimes known as the lesser burnet, this is common on the dry, chalky soils of pastures, waste places and railway banks in all parts of England. It has spikes of pink and green flowers, carried singly well above the foliage rather

like thrift, and the leaves are most attractive. Great burnet (*S. officinalis*) is a much taller-growing relative with larger, deep crimson flowers and grows mainly in damp meadows.

In the garden, salad burnet grows to about 45cm (18in) and apart from needing good drainage, is very tolerant of situation. Possibly the best spot for it is in a herb garden together with the thymes, sages and other sun-loving herbs, but it also makes a colourful plant for the front of a mixed border. The graceful, fern-like leaves look very effective drooping over paving and are evergreen throughout a mild winter.

There is also a rather spectacular cultivated garden burnet, *S. canadensis*. It originated in North America, has white cylindrical flowers up to 15cm (6in) long, similar fern-like leaves and grows up to 1.2–1.5m (4–5ft).

As a herb salad burnet is grown chiefly for the leaves, which are slightly bitter but fresh and cooling and with a taste resembling cucumber. It is a useful ingredient in small quantities in a salad, especially in winter. An infusion can be drunk as a tonic or used on the skin against sunburn.

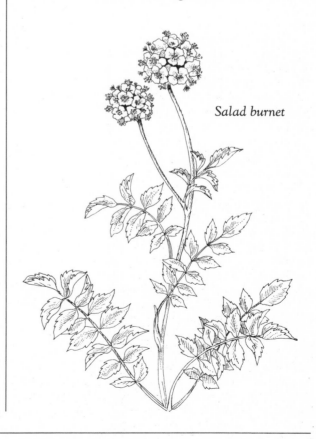

Salad burnet

Plants like this navelwort can be introduced into walls with natural crevices.

Selfheal

◆ SELFHEAL ◆

Prunella vulgaris

Flowering season	◆ June to September
Soil	◆ normal border
Acidity	◆ neutral/acid
Situation	◆ sun/partial shade
Propagation	◆ seed/division

This is a native low-growing perennial plant of grassland, wasteland, hedgerows and roadsides common throughout Britain except the north of Scotland. In parts of Europe it is a widespread lawn weed but is less of a problem in this country.

The name selfheal comes from the wide range of medical treatments for which it has been found effective. Other local names are 'sicklewort' and 'touch-and-heal'. The early settlers are supposed to have exported it to North America, where it is commonly called 'woundwort'.

For the garden selfheal provides a very good form of ground cover plant and the flowers are most attractive. It forms a mass of runners covered in leaves which send up square-shaped stems to about 30cm (12in) carrying a bunch of purple-blue flowers, shaped rather like a small antirrhinum. An uncultivated form found in the wild is actually a different species. Selfheal grows well either in the front of a border or on a grassy bank, but it can be smothered by tall grasses.

Selfheal is very attractive to bees, butterflies and other insects. Medically, the main treatments have been as a wash or styptic for external wounds and bruises, as a gargle against colds and catarrh and taken as a tea against internal bleeding. It was also said to purify the liver.

◆ SNOWDROP ◆

Galanthus nivalis

Flowering season	◆ January to March
Soil	◆ normal border/moist
Acidity	◆ acid/alkaline
Situation	◆ partial shade
Propagation	◆ seed/division

This is probably a native but even if it is not, the snowdrop has certainly been recorded in the wild for a very long time, growing in moist spots in woodlands and by streams, originally in Wales and south-west England. In other places it has escaped from cultivation. There are also several different cultivated forms of snowdrop grown in gardens, but the wild species has single flowers with short inner petals tipped with green.

Snowdrops have the reputation for being difficult to grow but in the right soil they should be very easy and once established spread very quickly. They need a moist soil throughout the year and usually seem to grow well on heavy clay, but lighter soils need peat or leaf mould working into them. Snowdrops also need shade, especially in summer, and dislike being planted in full sun. Short grass under trees also seems to suit them but this must not be cut until the foliage has died down. They grow to a height of about 20cm (8in).

Another spring-flowering relative is spring snowflake (*Leucojum vernum*) which grows quite widely, though rather scattered, in several English and Scottish localities. It is slightly taller than snowdrop and flowers a little later with smaller, white blooms and larger leaves. There is also a summer snowflake (*L. aestivum*), also called the Loddon lily, which is a native but only grows in a small area of southern England.

Snowdrop

◆ SOAPWORT ◆

Saponaria officinalis

Flowering season ◆ June to September	
Soil ◆ normal border	
Acidity ◆ neutral	
Situation ◆ sun	
Propagation ◆ seed, stratification advised/division	

The lack of other British species helps the belief that this is not a true native but was introduced many years ago from central and southern Europe as a cleaning agent for the wool trade. It escaped from being grown in fields around the wool factories and is now found growing quite widely under hedges and along roadsides, mainly in England and Wales.

Soapwort makes a splendid garden flower. Growing to about 90cm (3ft), it is an upright plant with attractive foliage and bunches of large pearly-pink flowers which brighten any border in late summer. It is best grown in a clump but as the strong roots can make it invasive, soapwort is a good plant for poorer, though fairly moist, garden soils or put with other vigorous growers like the Michaelmas daisies and golden-rod. It also succeeds well in the grass underneath a sunny hedgerow, where it spreads very quickly. Root division in winter is probably the best way to propagate it.

In addition to the stems being boiled to make a mild soapy solution, still sometimes used today to clean delicate fabrics and tapestries, soapwort has also had a number of medical uses in the past. These included internal treatments for coughs, colds and asthma and externally for skin inflammation, itching, cramp and rheumatism.

Soapwort

Spring gentian

◆ SPRING GENTIAN ◆

Gentiana verna

Flowering season ◆ June	
Soil ◆ normal border	
Acidity ◆ alkaline	
Situation ◆ sun	
Propagation ◆ seed, stratification advised	

This is a native perennial British 'alpine', growing in a very few grassy places on limestone in northern England and western Ireland. It is a protected plant and must not be picked, but it is much more widespread in European alpine countries.

Spring gentian typically blooms a real 'gentian blue', though there are pale blue and white variations, and makes a superb spring-flowering plant for a sunny, limestone-based rock garden. It grows to only about 5cm (2in) and can also be established in thin turf over chalk.

The marsh gentian (*G. pneumonanthe*) grows to about 30cm (12in) and is a lowland species, confined mainly to a few wet heathlands in south-east England and Wales. It is perennial and blooms in August and September with blue flowers and very narrow leaves. It needs moisture and sun and thrives in a mini-marsh or beside a sunny pond.

Also flowering late summer and autumn are the closely related felworts, sometimes called gentians but with the botanical name *Gentianella*. The Common felwort (*G. amarella*) grows up to about 30cm (12in) and is a biennial found on chalky downs throughout Britain except Scotland. It has a number of subspecies, all coloured purple or purple-red. Field felwort (*G. campestris*) is a purple annual species more common in Scotland.

◆ SWEET CICELY ◆

Myrrhis odorata

Flowering season ◆ **May to June**	
Soil ◆ **normal border**	
Acidity ◆ **neutral/alkaline**	
Situation ◆ **sun/partial shade**	
Propagation ◆ **seed, stratification advised/division**	

This perennial flowering herb may not be a true native but was undoubtedly introduced a long time ago. It is now quite common under hedges, along roadsides and in woods and pastures in northern Britain, though rarer elsewhere. It looks rather like a scented cow parsley, to which it is closely related, and other local names are anise fern and great chervil.

In addition to being planted in the herb garden, sweet cicely is well worth a place in the ornamental garden. It prefers partial shade and a moist soil and will grow up to 90cm (3ft). It makes a good plant for the shady rear of a mixed border and, unlike some other members of the family, is not too aggressive. The flat-headed umbels of white flowers and fern-like leaves are aromatic and attractive to bees and other insects.

Cow parsley (*Anthriscus sylvestris*) is one of the other white-flowering members of the same family, prolific along roadsides and on banks throughout most of Britain. The slightly shorter wild carrot (*Daucus carota*), common on waste places, and the even shorter pignut (*Conopodium majus*) or earthnut are both rather more suitable for growing under hedges or in sunny spare corners of a garden.

Sweet cicely has many herbal uses, including drying the fruits to use as a flavouring and chopping the leaves for salads or adding to cooked gooseberries and rhubarb as an alternative sweetener. Medically, the cooked roots have been claimed to relieve indigestion.

Sweet cicely

◆ SWEET VIOLET ◆

Viola odorata

Flowering season ◆ **February to April**	
Soil ◆ **normal border**	
Acidity ◆ **neutral/alkaline**	
Situation ◆ **sun/partial shade**	
Propagation ◆ **seed/division**	

One of the earliest flowering of our native wild plants, the sweet violet is very widespread on banks and in open woodland on chalky soils throughout much of southern Britain. Further north it is rather rare.

This is the purple, sometimes white, perfumed violet, though the name might come from a medieval association with modesty rather than the scent. It has long been grown as a garden plant and there are some cultivated forms. It seems more tolerant of soils than in the wild and can be grown as a plant for the front of a border, in short grass under a hedge or even in quite wet conditions. The related dog-violet is dealt with on page 76.

Sweet violet grows to about 15cm (6in) and in very sheltered conditions will often start to flower early in the new year. It spreads rapidly and can be propagated easily from rooting runners in the summer or splitting plants in the winter. Rather interestingly, there is a second crop of minute flowers carried under the leaves in the autumn which look like seedpods. They often set seed, which germinates best when sown immediately it is ripe. Sweet violet also makes a useful winter-flowering houseplant.

Early-flying insects benefit from the nectar of the sweet violet and it is a food plant for the caterpillars of some butterflies. The flowers were once widely used for their fragrance in cooking or to decorate a salad, while crystallised violets were a favourite medieval sweetmeat.

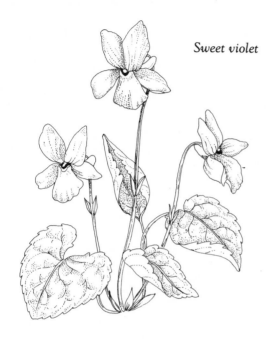

Sweet violet

·TANSY·

Tanacetum vulgare

Flowering season ◆ **June to September**	
Soil ◆ **normal border**	
Acidity ◆ **acid/alkaline**	
Situation ◆ **sun/partial shade**	
Propagation ◆ **seed/division**	

This is a native perennial found in the wild throughout most of Britain in hedgerows, waste places and along the roadside. Once a widely used garden herb, it is closely related to feverfew and also the varieties of garden matricaria developed as dwarf edging plants. An alternative name is 'bachelor's-buttons'.

In addition to the herb garden, tansy is well worth growing as a decorative plant in its own right. In good garden soil it will grow to 90cm (3ft) but often is rather shorter. It tolerates either full sun or partial shade and the masses of small, bright yellow flowers, or 'buttons', are combined with very luxuriant, dark green fern-like foliage. The native tansy is rather invasive and spreads very quickly, so it is best planted in a wild garden with other vigorous plants to help control it. For a mixed border it is better to grow a cultivated variety known as crisp-leaved tansy, which is shorter and not so vigorous.

Tansy was a popular herb and the name comes from a term used for herb-flavoured omelettes and puddings, sometimes eaten to break a lenten fast at Easter. It was used externally to clear the complexion and a poultice of leaves was applied to aches, sprains and varicose veins. The aroma made it a good plant for strewing as a deterrent of fleas, flies and, when hung in bunches in the branches, the pests of fruit trees. The leaves and flowers make a yellow dye and can be cut when young for dried flower arrangements.

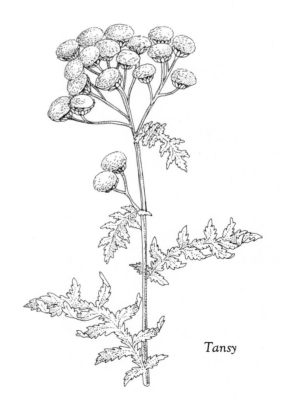

Tansy

Teasel

·TEASEL·

Dipsacus fullonum subsp. *sylvestris*

Flowering season ♦ **July to August**	
Soil ♦ **normal border/poor and dry**	
Acidity ♦ **neutral/alkaline**	
Situation ♦ **sun**	
Propagation ♦ **seed**	

This is a native biennial common on roadsides, the banks of rivers and canals and in dry pastures in the southern part of England but rather more rare elsewhere. It is not the same as the fuller's teasel, a subspecies (*fullonum*) once widely cultivated for raising the knap of cloth in the woollen industry, but is closely related to it. There is also a much more dainty relative scattered throughout the moist woodlands and ditches of Britain called the small teasel (*D. pillosus*), but this is shorter and with a smaller flowering head.

Teasel is a most stately plant to grow in the garden. Although the small, purple flowers only bloom for a short period, the prickly heads on tall stems are attractive throughout autumn and winter and make an easily-dried indoor winter flower arrangement. Being biennial, in the first year the seedlings make a flattened rosette of leaves which over-winter and the spikes grow up during the second season. As these can grow up to 1.8m (6ft) in good soil, teasel needs placing carefully. The best site is often on a dry bank, where it will not grow so high but the many seedlings can be more easily controlled.

Teasel attracts a range of wildlife to its flowers, though small insects often drown in pools of water formed by the cup-shaped bracts on the stems. This led to the erroneous belief that the plant was carnivorous. The flowers attract the humble bee and many butterflies, including the common blue and small copper, while in autumn goldfinches feed on the seeds.

·THRIFT·

Armeria maritima subsp. *maritima*

Flowering season ♦ **April to August**	
Soil ♦ **normal border/poor and dry**	
Acidity ♦ **acid/alkaline**	
Situation ♦ **sun/partial shade**	
Propagation ♦ **seed/cuttings**	

Thrift

Although a widely grown and popular garden plant, this is a true native and grows very widely throughout Britain. Basically a maritime plant, hence the alternative name of sea-pink, it grows on dunes, salt marshes, cliffs and tidal areas but also can be found on mountains inland. The usual colour is rose-pink but it can vary and there are a number of red, pink and white cultivated forms. There are also some other subspecies growing locally in places like Jersey.

In good garden soil thrift will make a cushion over 30cm (12in) across, with the flowering stems also growing up to about 30cm (12in), but grown on a dry site like a path edging it will not grow so wide or tall. It also grows well on a rockery or in paving and even as an edging for a pond or stream. Here the soil must be well drained but, as with tides by the sea, it will stand frequent flooding. When grown by the sea, thrift tolerates any amount of salt spray in either summer or winter, and is a good plant to grow in a hilly, windy area.

Thrift produces plenty of nectar and the multitude of flowers attract bees and butterflies for much of the summer.

Common sea-lavender (*Limonium vulgare*) is a fairly close relative which grows naturally in muddy salt marshes and is another suitable plant for sunny, seaside gardens. It is slightly taller than thrift and needs a moist, fertile soil.

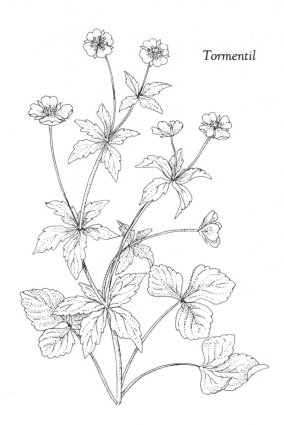

Tormentil

◆ TORMENTIL ◆

Potentilla erecta

Flowering season ◆ **May to October**	
Soil ◆ **normal border/moist**	
Acidity ◆ **neutral/acid**	
Situation ◆ **sun**	
Propagation ◆ **seed/division/cuttings**	

This native perennial with yellow strawberry-like flowers grows very widely in moist meadows, mountains, heaths and bogland throughout Britain. There are separate erect and more trailing species. The name comes from the Latin for colic, against which the roots were once recommended. It is a close relative of the cultivated garden potentillas.

In the garden tormentil grows up to about 50cm (20in), with the bright yellow flowers carried on slender stems which also have five-lobed leaves. It is seen at its best on a sunny moist bank, the edge of a pond or even in the moist pockets of a rockery. It also likes a peaty mini-marsh but it must not be over-grown by taller plants.

A close relative of tormentil is silver weed (*P. anserina*). This also likes moist soil and is common on roadsides throughout much of Britain, where it seems to thrive on the mud and water thrown up by traffic, though it will rarely be found where the soil is very dry. Although it has similar yellow flowers to tormentil, the attraction of silver weed is the bright silver basal leaves, also known as Prince of Wales' feathers, which make it a handsome plant to naturalise on a grassy garden bank.

'Blood-root' is another name given to tormentil and refers to the red dye made from the juice of the roots, once also used for tanning in place of oak bark. A tincture was also recommended against fevers.

◆ TRAVELLER'S-JOY ◆

Clematis vitalba

Flowering season ◆ **July to August**	
Soil ◆ **normal border/poor and dry**	
Acidity ◆ **alkaline**	
Situation ◆ **sun/partial shade**	
Propagation ◆ **seed/cutting**	

This is our only native clematis, though it was crossed with an imported species to make a rather lovely garden hybrid. Often more commonly known as old-man's-beard, in the wild it grows on chalky soil in mainly southern England and Wales and climbs over hedgerows, scrub and the edge of woodlands to often cover them with the sticky, woolly seedheads in autumn and early winter.

As the stems of traveller's-joy have been measured over 30m (100ft) in length, this is not a wild flower to plant in a small garden. An ideal situation is to let it ramble over a large, untrimmed hedge or an old, derelict apple or plum tree. Like all clematis, it will stand dry soil but likes to have roots in the shade and flowers in the sun so if you must plant it in a sunny position, place slates or tiles on top of the rooting area.

Though not individually very large, the greeny-white flowers of traveller's-joy are quite pretty and grow in great abundance. The leaves are a quite striking dark green and carried in opposite pairs on the stems, five leaflets to each. As well as growing up, the stems also trail down and along so this helps weed control in a hedge bottom.

Together with other climbing plants such as wild hop (*Humulus lupulus*), traveller's-joy makes a good garden sanctuary and nesting site for a number of the smaller birds.

Traveller's-joy

◆ VIPER'S-BUGLOSS ◆

Echium vulgare

Flowering season ◆ **June to September**	
Soil ◆ **normal border/poor and dry**	
Acidity ◆ **neutral/alkaline**	
Situation ◆ **sun**	
Propagation ◆ **seed**	

Viper's-bugloss is a native biennial which is commonly found in the east and south-east of England on the edge of cultivated fields, on sand dunes, cliffs and other dry places and occasionally elsewhere. It is a member of the borage family, which includes alkanet, the forget-me-nots and hound's-tongue. It can become a troublesome weed if allowed to seed on dry soils. The name comes from a supposed resemblance between the seed and a snake's head, though it has been claimed the plant is a specific against snake-bite.

In the garden viper's-bugloss seems less fussy about soil and makes a good garden plant, provided it is grown in sunshine. It produces masses of bright blue flowers carried on long stems growing up to about 75cm (30in), and streaked with purple. It is suitable for a mixed border but is also vigorous enough to grow in a wild garden where, although a biennial, it will self-seed itself quite easily every year. It is only suitable for a flowering meadow on light soils.

Viper's-bugloss

There are about ten native species of forget-me-nots, plus all the cultivated forms which make excellent spring bedding plants. Some are annual and others perennial but all self-seed so easily that once established they should keep going for ever. The name could be a reflection of this tenacity but a much older title was scorpion grass.

Water forget-me-not

Viper's-bugloss is an outstanding plant for attracting bees and other insects like hover-flies, butterflies and moths. It can be used in similar ways to the non-native borage, with the young leaves put in salads or cooked like spinach. The flowers make a culinary decoration and can also be used to make a cooling summer drink. Being rich in minerals, it has been claimed that the leaves have a number of healing properties, including an infusion drunk against coughs and bronchitis or inhaled as a vapour.

WATER
◆ FORGET-ME-NOT ◆

Myosotis scorpioides

Flowering season ◆ **May to September**	
Soil ◆ **moist**	
Acidity ◆ **acid/alkaline**	
Situation ◆ **partial shade/shade**	
Propagation ◆ **seed/division**	

The water forget-me-not is one of the prettiest species and is fairly common in the wild. In the garden it grows to a height of about 30cm (12in) and is best planted on the shady side of a pond, where the clear blue flowers with yellow centres and strap-shaped leaves form a delicate contrast to other water plants. Two other moisture-loving species are the much lower-growing creeping forget-me-not (M. *secunda*) and tufted forget-me-not (M. *laxa*), both fairly common in damp places.

Field forget-me-not (M. *arvensis*) is a common weed of agricultural land and can become an awful pest in the garden if allowed to seed and colonise. It grows about 30cm (12in) tall. Rather prettier, slightly taller and a better plant for the wild garden is the wood forget-me-not (M. *sylvatica*). This is a true perennial and, despite its name, will also grow in an open border as well as in semi-shade. It grows into more of a clump, rather like the cultivated sorts, and makes a good edging plant. The flowers have an orange ring in the centre. Most unusual of all is the dwarf changing forget-me-not (M. *discolor*), with tiny flowers which open yellow and change to blue.

· WELD ·

Reseda luteola

Flowering season ◆ **June to August**	
Soil ◆ **normal border**	
Acidity ◆ **neutral/alkaline**	
Situation ◆ **sun**	
Propagation ◆ **seed**	

Weld is a native biennial common on roadsides, field edges and waste ground on chalky soils throughout much of Britain except the far north. It was very widely cultivated as a source of yellow dye, which gave the alternative name of dyer's-rocket.

Weld makes a most handsome garden plant and deserves to be more widely planted. In the second year after sowing it produces a flower spike up to 1.5m (5ft) tall on good soil, not unlike a taller yellow foxglove but with a mass of much smaller flowers and a mass of narrow, green leaves. It is a good plant for the rear of a sunny border but also looks good grown on its own against a background of trees. Although biennial, it self-sets seed easily.

A very similar plant and a very close relation to weld is wild mignonette (*R. lutea*). This is a different species to the very fragrant mignonette grown in gardens, which comes from north Africa, but can also be a good plant for the garden, growing to no more than half the height of weld. Naturally it grows as a weed of cultivated ground and waste places throughout England and Wales, but in the garden it forms a good constituent of a mini-meadow and is very attractive to butterflies and bees. The flowers are creamy-yellow and the leaves more toothed than weld. There is also a white form, but this is a different species and almost certainly not a native. Both make very fragrant cut flowers.

Welsh poppy

Weld

· WELSH POPPY ·

Meconopsis cambrica

Flowering season ◆ **June to August**	
Soil ◆ **moist**	
Acidity ◆ **acid**	
Situation ◆ **sun/partial shade**	
Propagation ◆ **seed**	

The most vigorous of our perennial native poppies, this grows naturally on damp, rocky sites through much of Wales and in parts of south-west England. It has also become a popular garden plant and has now escaped into the wild in a number of other moist areas.

In the garden the Welsh poppy grows to about 60cm (2ft) with pretty, yellow flowers and delicate foliage, similar to the popular Iceland poppy but rather greener. There is also an orange form seen mostly in gardens. Welsh poppy will often succeed best under high shade in a shrubbery, but it tolerates sun provided the soil is kept moist and the site is sheltered. It is intolerant of lime but grows well in a moist pocket of a rock garden.

Welsh poppy is not easy to raise as it dislikes being split up or transplanted and must be grown from seed. Germination can be very slow and erratic so this is one plant where seedboxes need leaving in a damp corner, often for several months, until seedlings are through. Once growing on a site it likes, it will then self-seed quite happily.

Other colourful poppies found growing in the wild include the lilac form of the annual opium poppy (*Papaver somniferum*), not a native but once cultivated for seed-oil and now escaped, and two other annual species often mistaken for the common red poppy but lacking its distinctive dark centre.

◆ WHITE CAMPION ◆

Silene alba

Flowering season ◆ **May to August**	
Soil ◆ **normal border**	
Acidity ◆ **acid/alkaline**	
Situation ◆ **sun/meadow**	
Propagation ◆ **seed**	

A native short-lived perennial, white campion is common on roadsides, waste places and cultivated land throughout most of Britain. It is not generally such a vigorous plant as red campion or quite so tall and flowers slightly later. A pink hybrid between the two is fairly common where they grow together.

S. pendula is a dwarf close relative from south-

ern Europe with single and double forms quite widely grown as a rockery plant. It has a strong carnation-like scent and although the species is white, pink and carmine shades have also been bred.

In the evenings white campion is also scented, though this fades during the day. To get the full effect from the pure white flowers it needs planting in a fairly large clump, either in a sunny mixed flower border or with red campion and other native flowers in a wild garden. In good soil it can grow up to nearly 90cm (3ft) but it tolerates quite dry, poor conditions, where the plants will not grow so high and the flowers are often seen at their best. It also grows well in a flowering meadow.

As the name suggests, sea campion (*S. maritima*) is a native of the seaside and grows on cliffs, shingle banks and rocks throughout the country and sometimes on mountains inland. It seldom grows to more than about 20cm (8in), is white in colour and grows well in a rock garden, especially by the sea.

White campion

WILD
· DAFFODIL ·

Narcissus pseudonarcissus

Flowering season ◆ February to April	
Soil ◆ normal border/moist	
Acidity ◆ neutral/acid	
Situation ◆ sun/partial shade	
Propagation ◆ seed/division	

The original common wild native species, also known as Lent lily, was at one time distributed quite widely throughout England and Scotland but unknown elsewhere. Nowadays it still survives in a number of damp woodlands, parkland and moist meadows, though it often suffers from over-picking. There are a few other wild native species, like the Tenby daffodil (*N. obvallaris*) found in a small area of Dyfed, and any waste tip near houses will show plenty that have escaped from gardens.

In addition to the many cultivated types and varieties, there is a place in the garden for the wild daffodil. In height it grows somewhere between the tall garden hybrids and the miniatures and in good soil will usually reach about 40cm (16in). The flowers grow one per stem with creamy-yellow petals and a darker yellow trumpet.

Daffodils are best grown completely undisturbed, as in the wild, so a good place is a shrubbery with high growing deciduous shrubs, giving light shade when flowering but keeping the soil cool while the bulbs rest in summer. Wild daffodil will also make up into large clumps growing in grass which must not be cut until all the foliage has died.

Bulbs of the genuine wild daffodil can be bought from specialist seedsmen and nurseries and should be planted about 7cm (3in) deep in September.

Wild daffodil

WILD
· MARJORAM ·

Origanum vulgare

Flowering season ◆ July to September	
Soil ◆ normal border/poor and dry	
Acidity ◆ neutral/alkaline	
Situation ◆ sun	
Propagation ◆ seed/cuttings/division	

This is the native perennial marjoram, or oregano, and a close relative of other species imported many years ago as valuable herbs. It is common on dry banks, roadsides and in scrubland and pastures, on chalky soils throughout England and Wales, though rare elsewhere. A golden form is very popular in gardens and another local name is 'joy-of-the-mountain'.

Wild marjoram grows from a creeping rootstock and forms a bush which reaches 75cm (30in) and is covered in small leaves arranged in pairs. The flowers are small and pink but carried in large bunches. They are shaped rather like the mints, to which marjoram is related. Though it has herbal uses, wild marjoram is probably best placed at the front of a border in full sun where it will make a good ground cover. Unless grown in poor soil, wild marjoram spreads rapidly.

Another herbal relative is the pot or French marjoram which came originally from the mediterranean region but is hardy in most of this country in well-drained soils. Sweet marjoram (*O. marjorana*) is another import, more compact than either of the others and useful for a small herb garden.

One culinary use for marjoram is to flavour meat and other dishes. The leaves have been used with oil to cure toothache and rheumatism and stuffed into a pillow dried to help insomniacs.

Wild marjoram

Wild pansy

◆ WILD PANSY ◆

Viola tricolor

Flowering season ◆ April to September	
Soil ◆ normal border	
Acidity ◆ neutral/acid	
Situation ◆ sun/partial shade, meadow	
Propagation ◆ seed	

Often more commonly known as heart's-ease or other country names such as 'love-in-idleness', it was also called 'herb trinity' from the three-coloured face which gives the name to the species. These colours can vary but most common is a combination of purple, white and yellow. Heart's-ease can also cross with the field pansy, a widespread agricultural annual weed of limited garden value, to give some intermediate forms. The yellow-flowered mountain pansy is found only in the north of Britain and was used with the wild pansy to produce many hybrid garden pansies and violas.

Put in the right place, heart's-ease is equally as worth growing as garden pansies. Like them, it flowers for a long time if kept dead-headed and is tolerant of soils and situation. As a short-lived perennial it can be planted out in clumps at the front of the border, or left to seed itself and spread through a wild garden. It is also used as an ingredient of a flowering meadow to give colour in the first year. It reaches a height of about 30cm (12in) in good soil.

The name may come from treating either a medical heart condition or unrequited love and a tea made from the leaves was claimed to treat chest and lung infections, rheumatism and fevers. Heart's-ease is attractive to bees and other insects and has strongly marked guidelines on the petals.

WILD ◆ STRAWBERRY ◆

Fragaria vesca

Flowering season ◆ April to July	
Soil ◆ normal border	
Acidity ◆ neutral/alkaline	
Situation ◆ sun/partial shade	
Propagation ◆ seed/division	

This native species of a popular fruit grows widely throughout Britain in dry grassland and woods. It flowers over a longer season than cultivated strawberries and generally fruits from late June to August. It is closely related to cinquefoil and the herbaceous garden potentillas, both of which have a similar trailing habit. Some wild strawberries are actually seedlings from garden plants distributed through the droppings of birds while there is also a barren strawberry of woodlands which carries no fruit at all.

The wild strawberry is a very old garden plant and was the original source of fruit until the hybridised garden varieties were introduced from North America and Chile. Though small, the fruits are very sweet but unless netted, you might not get to eat them before the birds. Even without the fruit, this is a very handsome plant, with open white flowers carried partly free of bright green foliage which is greyer underneath. In good soil the plants grow to about 30cm (12in) but rather less when set in grass in a sunny hedgebottom.

In addition to being eaten, strawberry fruit juice has been used in the past as a remedy for sunburn, to remove skin blemishes and to strengthen teeth and gums, whilst strawberry tea was said to guard against fevers.

Wild strawberry

Wild thyme

· WILD THYME ·

Thymus praecox subsp. *arcticus*

Flowering season ◆ **May to August**	
Soil ◆ **poor and dry**	
Acidity ◆ **neutral/alkaline**	
Situation ◆ **sun**	
Propagation ◆ **seed/cuttings/division**	

This is one of the three thymes native to this country. It is also known as 'bank thyme', 'horse thyme' and 'shepherd's thyme', and grows on dry grassland on mainly chalky soils. It is more plentiful in the north and west than in the rest of Britain. The flavour is not so strong as the normal culinary thyme, a native of southern Europe, but the foliage is still very aromatic when crushed.

Wild thyme is now mainly planted in gardens as an ornamental, though sprigs were used for flavouring in the past and it will survive hard winters better than its imported cousin. Like all thymes, it is really a sub-shrub and can be used to clothe sunny banks or slopes with dense, wiry stems and partly evergreen foliage. It also grows well at the front of a border, where it will need controlling, in paving stones and even as an interesting small lawn. The height is from 10–30cm (4–12in) depending on situation, and the flowers are purply-white. There are some cultivated varieties.

Even lower growing is another native thyme only found in the wild in Breckland, part of Norfolk, where it grows in sandy heaths and grassland. The colour is pink but several garden varieties have been bred from it which are listed in catalogues under *T. serphyllum*. Both these and the original form are used widely for rock gardens, in paving and in patio containers. All thymes are very attractive to bees and other insects.

WILD
· WALLFLOWER ·

Cheiranthus cheiri

Flowering season ◆ **April to August**	
Soil ◆ **normal border/poor and dry**	
Acidity ◆ **neutral/alkaline**	
Situation ◆ **sun**	
Propagation ◆ **seed**	

Not a true native but it was introduced from southern Europe a long time ago. Wild wallflower is a short-lived perennial which is now naturalised very widely in the south of Britain, though in the north it is more rare. It flowers for a much longer period than the garden wallflowers, all bred from it, and is found growing out of walls, old ruins or in mainly rocky places. In the Middle Ages it was called the gillyflower and used in posies.

The flowers are yellow and carried in bunches on wiry stems which in good soil grow to 60cm (2ft), but less in very dry places. Although fragrant, the flowers do not have the concentration of scent of a bed of their cultivated relations, but outside the main flowering period occasional blooms will appear in almost any month of the year.

In the garden wild wallflower can be grown in beds but it self-seeds very easily and can soon get out of control. It might therefore be better to imitate nature and grow it in a sunny, dry corner, possibly to help clothe a heap of builder's rubble. It also grows well, but less high, in the crevices of an old wall or even in a rockery or scree bed.

Wild wallflower is attractive to butterflies and other insects, which benefit from the longer flowering season. An oil extracted from it, called cheirinum, was used in perfumery and as a remedy for the ague.

Wild wallflower

Winter aconite

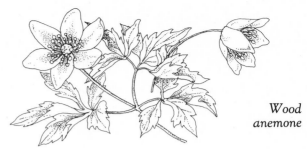

Wood anemone

◆ WINTER ACONITE ◆

Eranthis hyemalis

Flowering season ◆	**January to March**
Soil ◆	**normal border/moist**
Acidity ◆	**neutral**
Situation ◆	**partial shade/shade**
Propagation ◆	**seed/division**

Although not a true native, this early flowering bulb has been naturalised here for so long that the golden flowers are widely regarded as a first harbinger of spring – often with little justification! In the wild the winter aconite grows in moist woodlands and clearings, mainly in southern England though sometimes elsewhere as a more recent garden escape – such as old parkland.

The bulbs, actually small tubers, need planting in clumps of eight to ten at 6cm (2½in) deep in moist soil, well-supplied with either peat or leaf mould. Although winter aconite likes to flower in full sun, like most other early-flowering bulbs, for the rest of the year it needs cool and fairly heavy shade. The foliage lasts for some time after flowering but if left until it dies back naturally, the plants should set seed and help the clumps to spread quite quickly. Another way to help increase them is to lift and split the tubers but this is best done immediately after flowering.

The true native aconite (*Aconitum napellus*), also called 'wolf's-bane' or 'monkshood', is really a different plant altogether, although it also lives in shady wet spots and on the banks of streams in Wales and south-west England. Together with several cultivated varieties it is grown quite widely as a garden plant, though all parts are poisonous, especially the root. It reaches about 90cm (3ft) in good soil and has bright blue flowers rather like a delphinium.

◆ WOOD ANEMONE ◆

Anemone nemorosa

Flowering season ◆	**March to May**
Soil ◆	**normal border/moist**
Acidity ◆	**acid/alkaline**
Situation ◆	**partial shade/shade**
Propagation ◆	**seed/division**

Also known as the windflower, this early-flowering native spreads by underground rhizomes and is very common in moist woodlands and hedges throughout Britain. The masses of single flowers are mainly white, flushed pink on the undersides with yellow stamens. There are also natural variations of blue and pink tinted flowers, some of which have been selected out for cultivation. The very popular *A. blanda* originated from the mountain wild flower of Greece.

In the garden wood anemone should be planted under deciduous trees or shrubs, where the tubers can rest in moisture and shade once they die down after flowering. The flowers close during the night and in wet and windy weather. In good soil they grow to about 25cm (10in) and the slender stems also carry three bright green, divided leaves.

Commonly associated with wood anemone in the wild is wood-sorrel (*Oxalis acetosella*). Although a member of the oxalis family, it blooms at about the same time and also likes shade and a moist soil. The flowers also are very similar, though usually rather whiter, but the three-part leaves are typically oxalis-shaped and have the unusual habit of closing up in bad weather or drought.

Local country names for wood-sorrel like 'bread-and-cheese' show the leaves were once eaten and by the fifteenth century it was cultivated for salads.

◆ WOOD AVENS ◆

Geum urbanum

Flowering season ◆ **May to August**	
Soil ◆ **normal border/moist**	
Acidity ◆ **acid/alkaline**	
Situation ◆ **partial shade/shade**	
Propagation ◆ **seed/division**	

This native perennial lives in damp soil in woodlands, hedgerows and other shady places over most of Britain except the north of Scotland. Another common name is herb-bennet, possibly a corruption of St. Benedict as it has also been known as the 'blessed-herb' for its powers of healing. It is closely related to both water avens and the cultivated garden geums, which are sometimes seen in the wild as garden escapes.

Wood avens has dainty yellow flowers carried on long slender stems carrying dark green foliage. In good soil it can grow up to 60cm (2ft) and is a useful plant for quite heavy, moist shade. Although it can be grown in a shady mixed border, it is at its best seen straggling under trees, where the dense foliage acts as a good ground cover.

Wood avens

Water avens is a plant for moist soil at the side of a pond or in a mini-marsh. It is best placed in shade but will also grow quite happily out into the sun. The flowers are a subtle purplish-orange tinged with pink and form most attractive seed-heads. It grows to about the same height as wood avens but the stem leaves are slightly smaller and more feathery.

The aromatic roots of wood avens smell of cloves and are said to have been used by the Romans as an alternative to quinine. The roots have also been used to cure digestive disorders and an infusion of the leaves for bronchitis and as an astringent tonic added to water for washing.

◆ WOODRUFF ◆

Galium odoratum

Flowering season ◆ **May to June**	
Soil ◆ **normal border/moist**	
Acidity ◆ **alkaline**	
Situation ◆ **partial shade/shade**	
Propagation ◆ **seed/division**	

Often known as sweet woodruff, this is a native perennial widespread in woods throughout Britain and in several other parts of the world. Closely related to the bedstraws and cleavers or goosegrass, its natural home in the woodlands may have given rise to other popular names like 'kiss-me-quick' and 'ladies-in-the-hay'. Both flowers and leaves are also scented and this helped to make it a useful country plant.

In the garden woodruff can be planted in dark corners which get little direct sunlight but stay reasonably moist during the summer. Both the brilliant white flowers and bright green foliage are star shaped and even after the rather short-lived flower season is over, the leaves provide useful ground cover. The plants grow to about 30cm (12in) in good soil but it will also grow quite well at the base of a tree and eventually cover quite a large soil area.

In addition to the dried, aromatic straw being used for scenting mattresses and stored linen and as an air-freshener like the bedstraws, woodruff has long had a number of culinary and medicinal

A well-established garden with plenty of sources of nectar should be full of a range of butterflies from spring until autumn. Here, an Essex skipper can be seen on a scentless mayweed flower-head.

uses. The fresh leaves can be steeped in apple juice or a home-made flower wine like elderflower, or dried and made into a soothing tea said to be good for headaches, insomnia and migraine. Conversely, it was also said to be exhilarating and to encourage a spirit of *joie de vivre* – possibly this is the true origin of the names like 'kiss-me-quick'!

Woodruff

◆ WOOD SPURGE ◆

Euphorbia amygdaloides

Flowering season ◆ March to May
Soil ◆ normal border/moist
Acidity ◆ neutral/alkaline
Situation ◆ shade
Propagation ◆ seed

This is a native member of a very large family which includes a number of cultivated plants and some succulents grown as house plants. Wood spurge is an herbaceous perennial which lives in the deep shade of old deciduous woodlands and clearings and is common in England and Wales. The stems grow to about 60cm (2ft), have dark green leaves and are topped by several stemlets each carrying one or more greeny-yellow 'flowers'. Like other members of the family, these are actually large bracts with the small flowers, more yellow than green, carried inside them.

Wood spurge is ideal to plant under trees or in other heavy shade where little else will flower. The large heads of bright leaf bracts will brighten up any dark corner and it makes a good background to other spring-flowering woodland-type flowers and bulbs. It likes a moist soil in spring, so incorporate peat or leaf mould before planting, but tolerates otherwise dry conditions and summers.

Other native members of the family include the sun spurge (*E. helioscopia*), which is annual and a fairly common weed of cultivated ground, and the biennial caper spurge (*E. lathyrus*) with large leaves and fruits rather like a caper. This is possibly not a native to this country but is found widely in gardens where it has been used to deter moles. The dwarf spurge (*E. exigua*) is another annual which flowers quite late into autumn. Most spurges have a milky sap which has been used to treat warts but can cause a skin rash if not handled carefully.

Wood spurge

The large, voracious caterpillars of the mullein moth devour the equally large, woolly leaves of the great mullein.

Yarrow

◆ YARROW ◆

Achillea millefolium

Flowering season ◆ **June to November**	
Soil ◆ **normal border/poor and dry**	
Acidity ◆ **acid/alkaline**	
Situation ◆ **sun, meadow**	
Propagation ◆ **seed/division**	

A very common wayside flower, this thrives in waste places, dry grassland, hedges and in gardens throughout Britain. The Latin name is said to be derived from its use in treating wounds at the time of Achilles, while its later use as an astringent gave other common names like 'nosebleed' and 'carpenter's-weed'. It is also sometimes called the milfoil.

Although yarrow can become a weed of lawns, a number of cultivated species, varieties and hybrids of Achillea are widely grown as tall herbaceous plants for the rear of a border. There are also other imported species of various shapes and colours while another native, commonly called sneezewort (*A. ptarmica*), is a useful, though rather aggressive, white-flowered garden plant.

Grown in good soil, yarrow will reach 90cm (3ft) and makes an attractive clump for a mixed flower border, though it will need regular thinning. It is rather more controllable in a flowering meadow, where it does not grow so tall. The flowers, which range from white through to pale shades of pink, red and cerise, form a bright contrast to the grasses and stand quite frequent cutting.

Like all the tall achilleas, yarrow is good for cutting fresh and for winter flower arrangement. The stems should be harvested while the flowers are still young and hung in the dry with heads downwards.

YELLOW ◆ ARCHANGEL ◆

Lamiastrum galeobdolon

Flowering season ◆ **May to June**	
Soil ◆ **normal border/moist**	
Acidity ◆ **alkaline/acid**	
Situation ◆ **partial shade/shade**	
Propagation ◆ **seed/division**	

This is possibly the most colourful of the very widespread dead-nettle family. In the wild it grows in moist woodlands, clearings and sheltered belts and is common in southern and central England but more rare elsewhere. The name dead-nettle

Yellow archangel

comes from a superficial resemblance of the leaves to nettles but they do not sting. Other country names for yellow archangel are 'yellow dead-nettle, dumb nettle' and 'stingy-wingles'.

In the garden yellow archangel succeeds in either light or heavy shade but it needs a moist, fertile soil to grow well. It reaches about 60cm (2ft) on good soil. The flowers are bright yellow with attractive orange-brown centres and carried on square stems covered with a large number of fleshy, green leaves. It is best seen in the shady part of a mixed wild garden, rather than a border, where the other plants will help control its often rather rampant growth.

A similar wild situation suits the related white dead-nettle (*Lamium album*), which is another handsome plant but is rather invasive and often becomes a nuisance in a vegetable garden. It flowers for very much longer than yellow archangel, starting in March and often still showing a few blooms until Christmas. It needs full sun and flowers best in a poor, dry soil.

The annual red dead-nettle (*L. purpureum*) is sometimes known as the purple archangel. It has a long flowering season and will seed itself down in any waste corner.

YELLOW-HORNED ◆POPPY◆

Glaucium flavum

Flowering season ◆ **June to August**	
Soil ◆ **poor and dry**	
Acidity ◆ **neutral**	
Situation ◆ **sun**	
Propagation ◆ **seed**	

A native short-lived perennial growing in sands and gravels by the seaside everywhere in Britain except the north of Scotland. It has golden-yellow or sometimes orange flowers with fleshy, silvery foliage and the stems give a yellow dye when crushed. There is also a much smaller, annual red-horned poppy which is not a native but introduced and found only around seaports.

The yellow-horned poppy is grown quite widely in gardens and is very useful at the seaside, where it

withstands salt-laden winds. Inland it may not be so hardy but is worth trying on a light, well-drained soil. Planted in moist sand or gravel it will grow to about 60cm (2ft); often rather taller in better soils. The flowers are followed by even more striking seedpods which grow up to 30cm (12in) long.

Another good plant for seaside gardens is the burnet-rose (*Rosa pimpinellifolia*). This is a native low-growing shrub fairly common around the coasts except in the south-east of England. The flowers are mainly creamy-white, though sometimes pink, bloom from May to July followed by purple hips in the autumn and are sweetly scented.

Sea-buckthorn (*Hippophae rhamnoides*) is a shrub for larger seaside gardens. A native of the east coast, it has been widely planted around Britain to help stabilise sand dunes. It grows to a height of 2–3m (6–9ft), is covered with thorns and the flowers are green followed by a mass of orange berries in autumn.

Yellow-horned poppy

◆ YELLOW IRIS ◆

Iris pseudacorus

Flowering season ◆ **May to July**	
Soil ◆ **moist**	
Acidity ◆ **acid/alkaline**	
Situation ◆ **sun/partial shade**	
Propagation ◆ **seed, stratification advised/division**	

Alternatively known as the flag iris or yellow-flag, this is a 'must' for the margin of any pond or stream. In the wild it grows throughout Britain in marshes and wet grounds in ditches and by rivers, where its bright yellow flowers and blade-like leaves provide the local name of sword flower.

The yellow iris is one of the irises which grow from rhizomes, part under and part above ground, and by a small pond can be kept under control by thinning these regularly. It usually grows about 90cm (3ft) tall and will only flower well in either full sun or light shade. Even without flowers, the leaves make it a very handsome plant up which the nymphs of damsels and other water insects can climb and emerge into the sun.

In addition to planting it by a pond or stream, flag iris also makes a striking plant for a boggy part of the wild garden. There are a number of cultivated varieties, some with variegated foliage.

The so-called stinking iris (*I. foetidissima*), or gladdon, is another good native iris species, fairly common in hedgebanks, damp woods and sometimes on cliffs by the sea in southern England. The name is quite unfair as it is the roots that smell, not the flowers. These are pinkish-purple tinged with yellow but the great attraction are the large seedheads, which turn back to display brilliant orange seeds lasting for much of the winter.

Yellow iris

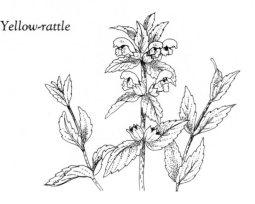

Yellow-rattle

◆ YELLOW-RATTLE ◆

Rhinanthus minor

Flowering season ◆ **May to August**	
Soil ◆ **poor and dry**	
Acidity ◆ **acid/alkaline**	
Situation ◆ **sun, meadow**	
Propagation ◆ **seed**	

This is an annual native which is semi-parasitic on grasses and found widely in dry meadows and on the roadside throughout Britain. It comes from an interesting family which includes the toadflaxes and has a rather similar flower. The name refers to the way seeds rattle in the seedpod when ripe. Other local names include 'baby's-rattles', 'rattle-penny' and 'money-grass'.

As yellow-rattle only grows with grasses, from which it takes water and nutrients by tapping the root systems, this bright yellow flower is used chiefly in the garden as a constituent of a flowering meadow, where it grows to about 45cm (18in).

The seed must be included in the meadow mixture when it is sown and not raised separately for later transplanting. However, it can be sown in a seedbox with a mixture of one part yellow-rattle to two parts of a suitable grass and the whole lot planted into a rough turf area once it has germinated. It also germinates much better in autumn than spring and although annual, once sown it will usually self-seed itself.

Two other plants that only grow in grass are pink lousewort (*Pedicularis sylvatica*) and the pretty white and purple eyebright (*Euphrasia officinalis*), which can both be raised in the same way.

WILD FLOWER
SELECTIONS

The following lists give a selection of useful wild flowers of different types for varying situations and uses. For more detailed information see the Guide to the 100 Most Suitable Wild Flowers (pages 69–132).

• Key to abbreviations

Small	– less than 30cm/1ft	
Medium	– between 30–60cm/1–2ft	Average heights in good garden soil
Tall	– over 60cm/2ft	
bf	– nectar plants for butterflies	
bd	– seed-producing plants for birds	
a	– annual	
b	– biennial	
p	– perennial	

• ANNUAL WILD FLOWERS FOR SUNNY BORDERS •

Plant name	Flowering	Colour	Height guide
Charlock *Sinapsis arvensis*	April–June	yellow	tall
Common field-speedwell *Veronica persica*	Feb–Oct	blue	small
Common fumitory *Fumaria officinalis*	May–Oct	purple	medium
Common poppy *Papaver rhoeas*	May–Aug	red	medium
Corn buttercup *Ranunculus arvensis*	June–July	yellow	medium
Corn chamomile *Anthemis arvensis*	June–July	white	small

Plant name	Flowering	Colour	Height guide
Corncockle *Agrostemma githago*	June–Aug	purple-pink	tall
Cornflower *Centaurea cyanus*	June–Aug	blue	tall, bf
Corn marigold *Chrysanthemum segetum*	June–Aug	yellow	medium, bf
Field forget-me-not *Myosotis arvensis*	April–Sept	blue	medium, bd
Field pansy *Viola arvensis*	April–Sept	cream	small
Ivy-leaved speedwell *Veronica hederifolia*	April–July	blue	small
Long-headed poppy *Papaver dubium*	June–July	red	medium
Pale flax *Linum bienne*	May–Sept	blue	medium, bd
Pheasant's-eye *Adonis annua*	May–July	red	medium
Scarlet pimpernel *Anagallis arvensis*	May–Aug	scarlet	small
Scented mayweed *Matricaria recutita*	May–Aug	white	medium
Scentless mayweed or chamomile *Tripleurospermum inodorum*	July–Sept	white	medium
White campion *Silene alba*	May–Aug	white	tall, bf
Wild pansy *Viola tricolor*	April–Sept	violet & yellow	small, bf

◆ BIENNIAL AND PERENNIAL FLOWERS ◆ FOR SUNNY BORDERS

Plant name	Flowering	Colour	Height guide	Type
Agrimony *Agrimonia eupatoria*	June–Aug	yellow	medium	compact, p
Alkanet *Anchusa officinalis*	June–Sept	blue	medium	bushy, p
Betony *Stachys officinalis*	June–Sept	purple	medium	bushy, p, bd
Bloody crane's-bill *Geranium sanguineum*	May–Aug	purple	medium	compact, p
Cheddar pink *Dianthus gratianopolitanus*	June–July	pink	small	clump-forming, p
Clustered bellflower *Campanula glomerata*	May–Sept	blue	small	leafy, p
Columbine *Aquilegia vulgaris*	May–June	blue	tall	open, p
Common comfrey *Symphytum officinale*	May–Sept	white, pink, blue	tall	large-leaved, p
Common dog-violet *Viola riviniana*	April–July	violet	small	spreading, p
Common evening-primrose *Oenothera biennis*	June–Sept	yellow	tall	large-leaved, b, bd
Common knapweed *Centaurea nigra*	June–Sept	purple	medium	loosely bushy, p, bd, bf
Common restharrow *Ononis repens*	June–Sept	pink	medium	spreading, p
Cowslip *Primula veris*	April–May	yellow	small	forms rosettes, p
Devil's-bit scabious *Succisa pratensis*	June–Oct	mauve	tall	open and erect, p, bf
Dusky crane's-bill *Geranium phaeum*	May–June	maroon	medium	large-leaved, compact, p

Plant name	Flowering	Colour	Height guide	Type
Elecampane *Inula helenium*	July–Aug	yellow	tall	large, erect, p
Feverfew *Tanacetum parthenium*	July–Aug	white	medium	loosely bushy, p, bf
Field scabious *Knautia arvensis*	June–Sept	mauve	tall	open, bushy, p, bf
Foxglove *Digitalis purpurea*	June–Sept	purple	tall	erect, b
Globeflower *Trollius europaeus*	June–Aug	yellow	medium	open, bushy, p
Goldenrod *Solidago virgaurea*	July–Sept	yellow	medium	erect, p
Greater celandine *Chelidonium majus*	May–July	yellow	tall	large-leaved, p, bf
Greater knapweed *Centaurea scabiosa*	July–Sept	purple	tall	open, bushy, p, bd, bf
Greater stitchwort *Stellaria holostea*	April–June	white	medium	compact, p
Great mullein *Verbascum thapsus*	June–Aug	yellow	tall	erect, b
Harebell *Campanula rotundifolia*	July–Sept	blue	small	open, bushy, p
Hemp-agrimony *Eupatorium cannibinum*	July–Sept	pink	tall	compact, erect, p, bf
Hoary mullein *Verbascum pulverulentum*	June–July	yellow	tall	erect, b
Hoary plantain *Plantago media*	May–Aug	pink	small	forms rosettes, p, bd
Jacob's-ladder *Polemonium caeruleum*	May–July	blue	tall	erect, p
Lady's bedstraw *Galium verum*	June–Aug	yellow	medium	forms clumps, p
Meadow clary *Salvia pratensis*	June–July	blue	tall	erect, p

Plant name	Flowering	Colour	Height guide	Type
Meadow crane's-bill *Geranium pratense*	May–Sept	blue	tall	open, large-leaved, p
Meadowsweet *Filipendula ulmaria*	June–Aug	white	tall	open, bushy, p, bd
Musk mallow *Malva moschata*	June–Aug	pink	tall	loosely bushy, p, bf
Narrow-leaved everlasting-pea *Lathyrus sylvestris*	June–Aug	red	tall	climbing, p
Nettle-leaved bellflower *Campanula trachelium*	July–Sept	blue	tall	erect, p
Oxeye daisy *Leucanthemum vulgare*	May–Aug	white	tall	free-flowering bushy, p, bf
Perforate St John's-wort *Hypericum perforatum*	June–Sept	yellow	medium	erect, p
Purple-loosestrife *Lythrum salicaria*	June–Aug	purple	tall	erect spires, p, bf
Ragged-robin *Lychnis flos-cuculi*	May–June	red	tall	slender, erect, p, bf
Red campion *Silene dioica*	May–Nov	red	tall	erect, p, bf
Sainfoin *Onobrychis viciifolia*	May–Aug	pink	medium	open, bushy, p
Small scabious *Scabiosa columbaria*	June–Aug	mauve	medium	open, bushy, p, bf
Sneezewort *Achillea ptarmica*	July–Aug	white	tall	erect, p
Soapwort *Saponaria officinalis*	July–Sept	pink	tall	open, erect, p
Sweet violet *Viola odorata*	Feb–April	violet	small	spreading, p
Teasel *Dipsacus fullonum* subsp. *sylvestris*	July–Aug	mauve	tall	upright, striking seed-heads, b, bd, bf

Plant name	Flowering	Colour	Height guide	Type
Viper's-bugloss *Echium vulgare*	June–Sept	blue	tall	open, bushy, p
Water forget-me-not *Myosotis scorpioides*	May–Sept	blue	medium	compact, p
Wild strawberry *Fragaria vesca*	April–July	white	small	spreading, p

◆ BIENNIAL AND PERENNIAL WILD FLOWERS ◆ FOR LIGHT SHADE

Plant name	Flowering	Colour	Height guide	Type
Betony *Stachys officinalis*	June–Sept	purple	medium	bushy, p, bd
Bluebell *Hyacinthoides non-scriptus*	April–June	blue	medium	flowering bulb, bf
Common dog-violet *Viola riviniana*	April–July	violet	small	trailing, p
Cowslip *Primula veris*	April–May	yellow	small	forms rosettes, p, bf
Dark mullein *Verbascum nigrum*	June–Oct	yellow	tall	erect, b
Devil's-bit scabious *Succisa pratensis*	June–Oct	mauve	tall	open, erect, p, bf
Dog-rose *Rosa canina*	June–July	pink	tall	spreading shrub
Enchanter's-nightshade *Circaea lutetiana*	June–Aug	white	medium	leafy, p
Foxglove *Digitalis purpurea*	June–Sept	purple	tall	stately, p
Garlic mustard *Alliaria petiolata*	April–June	white	tall	large-leaved, b
Germander speedwell *Veronica chamaedrys*	March–July	blue	medium	spreading, p

Plant name	Flowering	Colour	Height guide	Type
Greater stitchwort *Stellaria holostea*	April–June	white	medium	spreading ground cover, p
Great mullein *Verbascum thapsus*	June–Aug	yellow	tall	erect, b
Ground-ivy *Glechoma hederacea*	March–May	blue	small	spreading, p
Hairy St John's-wort *Hypericum hirsutum*	July–Aug	yellow	tall	upright, p
Hedge woundwort *Stachys sylvatica*	May–Aug	purple	tall	erect, p
Honeysuckle *Lonicera periclymenum*	June–Sept	cream-pink	tall	rambling shrub
Lesser celandine *Ranunculus ficaria*	March–May	yellow	small	spreading, p, bf
Lords-and-ladies *Arum maculatum*	April–May	green	medium	upright, p
Oxlip *Primula elatior*	April–May	yellow	small	forms rosettes, p, bf
Ragged-robin *Lychnis flos-cuculi*	May–June	red	tall	slender, erect, p, bf
Ramsons *Allium ursinum*	April–June	white	medium	spreading, flowering bulb
Sanicle *Sanicula europaea*	May–Aug	pink	medium	upright, p
Stinking hellebore *Helleborus foetidus*	March–April	green	medium	p
Sweet violet *Viola odorata*	Feb–April	violet	small	spreading, p, bf
Teasel *Dipsacus fullonum* subsp. *sylvestris*	July–Aug	mauve	tall	upright, striking seedheads, b, bf, bd

Plant name	Flowering	Colour	Height guide	Type
Tufted vetch *Vicia cracca*	June–Aug	blue	tall	scrambling, p
White bryony *Bryonia dioica*	May–Sept	white	tall	climbing, p
Wild strawberry *Fragaria vesca*	April–July	white	small	rambling, p
Winter aconite *Eranthis hyemalis*	Jan–March	yellow	small	flowering bulb, p
Wood anemone *Anemone nemorosa*	March–May	white	small	spreading, p
Wood avens *Geum urbanum*	May–Aug	yellow	medium	spreading, p
Wood forget-me-not *Myosotis sylvatica*	May–July	blue	medium	compact, p
Wood sage *Teucrium scorodonia*	July–Sept	yellow	medium	spreading, p
Wood-sorrel *Oxalis acetosella*	April–June	white	small	spreading, p
Wood spurge *Euphorbia amygdaloides*	March–May	green	tall	open, bushy, p
Yellow archangel *Lamiastrum galeobdolon*	May–June	yellow	medium	leafy and spreading

◆ PERENNIAL WILD FLOWERS FOR MOIST CONDITIONS ◆

Plant name	Flowering	Colour	Height guide	Type
Brooklime *Veronica beccabunga*	May–Aug	blue	medium	prostrate, p
Common fleabane *Pulicaria dysenterica*	July–Sept	yellow	medium	upright, leafy, p
Cuckooflower *Cardamine pratensis*	April–July	pink	medium	compact, p, bf
Gipsywort *Lycopus europaeus*	June–Sept	pink	tall	spreading, p

Plant name	Flowering	Colour	Height guide	Type
Greater bird's-foot-trefoil *Lotus uliginosus*	June–Aug	yellow	medium	creeping, p, bf
Hemp-agrimony *Eupatorium cannabinum*	July–Sept	pink	tall	compact, erect, p, bf
Lesser spearwort *Ranunculus flammula*	May–Sept	yellow	tall	creeping, p
Marsh-marigold *Caltha palustris*	March–July	yellow	medium	compact
Marsh woundwort *Stachys palustris*	July–Sept	purple	tall	upright, p, bf
Meadow buttercup *Ranunculus acris*	April–May	yellow	tall	creeping, bf
Meadowsweet *Filipendula ulmaria*	June–Aug	white	tall	upright, bd
Musk *Mimulus moschatus*	July–Sept	yellow	medium	compact, p
Purple-loosestrife *Lythrum salicaria*	June–Aug	purple	tall	upright, p, bf
Ragged-robin *Lychnis flos-cuculi*	May–June	red	tall	slender, erect, p, bf
Water avens *Geum rivale*	April–July	pink-purple	medium	creeping, p
Water figwort *Scrophularia auriculata*	June–Sept	red	tall	upright, p
Water forget-me-not *Myosotis scorpioides*	May–Sept	blue	medium	compact, p
Water mint *Mentha aquatica*	July–Oct	lilac	tall	spreading, p, bf
Yellow iris *Iris pseudacorus*	May–July	yellow	tall	upright, p
Yellow loosestrife *Lysimachia vulgaris*	July–Aug	yellow	tall	upright, p

◆ WILD FLOWERS FOR MEADOWS ◆

Plant name	Flowering	Colour	Height guide	Type
Black medick *Medicago lupulina*	April–Aug	yellow	medium	annual
Cat's-ear *Hypochoeris radicata*	May–Sept	yellow	medium	perennial, bf
Clustered bellflower *Campanula glomerata*	May–Sept	blue	small	perennial
Common bird's-foot-trefoil *Lotus corniculatus*	May–Sept	yellow	small	perennial, bd, bf
Common knapweed *Centaurea nigra*	June–Sept	purple	medium	perennial, bd, bf
Common restharrow *Ononis repens*	June–Sept	pink	medium	perennial
Common sorrel *Rumex acetosa*	May–June	pink	tall	perennial
Common vetch *Vicia sativa*	April–Sept	purple	tall	annual
Cowslip *Primula veris*	April–May	yellow	small	perennial, bf
Cuckooflower *Cardamine pratensis*	April–July	pink	medium	perennial, bf
Dropwort *Filipendula vulgaris*	June–Aug	white	tall	perennial
Field scabious *Knautia arvensis*	June–Sept	mauve	tall	perennial
Germander speedwell *Veronica chamaedrys*	March–July	blue	small	perennial
Goat's-beard *Tragopogon pratensis*	June–July	yellow	medium	annual
Great burnet *Sanguisorba officinalis*	June–Sept	red	tall	perennial
Greater knapweed *Centaurea scabiosa*	July–Sept	purple	tall	perennial, bd, bf

Plant name	Flowering	Colour	Height guide	Type
Harebell *Campanula rotundifolia*	July–Sept	blue	small	perennial
Hoary plantain *Plantago media*	May–Aug	pink	small	perennial, bd
Horseshoe vetch *Hippocrepis comosa*	May–July	yellow	small	perennial
Kidney vetch *Anthyllis vulneraria*	May–Sept	yellow	medium	perennial, bf
Lady's bedstraw *Galium verum*	June–Aug	yellow	medium	perennial
Marsh-marigold *Caltha palustris*	March–July	yellow	medium	perennial
Meadow buttercup *Ranunculus acris*	April–May	yellow	tall	perennial, bf
Meadow crane's-bill *Geranium pratense*	May–Sept	blue	tall	perennial
Meadow saxifrage *Saxifraga granulata*	April–June	white	medium	perennial
Meadowsweet *Filipendula ulmaria*	June–Aug	white	tall	perennial, bd
Oxeye daisy *Leucanthemum vulgare*	May–Aug	white	tall	perennial, bf
Pepper-saxifrage *Silaum silaus*	June–Aug	yellow	medium	perennial
Perforate St John's-wort *Hypericum perforatum*	June–Sept	yellow	medium	perennial
Pignut *Conopodium majus*	May–July	white	medium	perennial
Ragged-robin *Lychnis flos-cuculi*	May–June	red	tall	perennial, bf
Ribwort plantain *Plantago lanceolata*	April–Aug	brown	medium	perennial
Rough hawkbit *Leontodon hispidus*	May–Sept	yellow	medium	perennial, bf

Plant name	Flowering	Colour	Height guide	Type
Sainfoin *Onobrychis viciifolia*	May–Aug	pink	medium	perennial
Salad burnet *Sanguisorba minor* subsp. *minor*	May–Aug	green	medium	perennial
Selfheal *Prunella vulgaris*	June–Sept	purple	medium	perennial
Small scabious *Scabiosa columbaria*	June–Aug	mauve	medium	perennial, bf
Tufted vetch *Vicia cracca*	June–Aug	blue	tall	perennial
Weld *Reseda luteola*	June–Aug	yellow	tall	biennial
White campion *Silene alba*	May–Aug	white	tall	annual, bf
Wild basil *Clinopodium vulgare*	July–Sept	purple	medium	perennial
Wild carrot *Daucus carota* subsp. *carota*	June–Aug	white	tall	biennial
Wild mignonette *Reseda lutea*	May–Aug	yellow	medium	biennial
Yarrow *Achillea millefolium*	June–Nov	white	medium	perennial, bf
Yellow-rattle *Rhinanthus minor*	May–Aug	yellow	medium	annual

◆ OUTSTANDING BUTTERFLY NECTAR PLANTS ◆

Plant name	Flowering	Colour	Height guide	Type
Bird's-foot-trefoil *Lotus corniculatus*	May–Sept	yellow	small	p, bd
Bramble *Rubus fruticosus*	June–Aug	white	tall	sprawling shrub, p
Brown knapweed *Centaurea jacea*	July–Sept	purple	medium	open, bushy, p, bd

Above Since bee keeping has declined owing to a combination of factors, the wild bee has become more important. Here, a bumble bee extracts pollen from a yellow-rattle. *Below* A honey bee investigates a comfrey flower-head.

Plant name	Flowering	Colour	Height guide	Type
Bugle *Ajuga reptans*	May–July	blue	small	trailing, p
Cat's-ear *Hypochoeris radicata*	May–Sept	yellow	medium	p
Chicory *Cichorium intybus*	July–Oct	blue	tall	erect, p
Common fleabane *Pulicaria dysenterica*	July–Sept	yellow	medium	upright, leafy
Common knapweed *Centaurea nigra*	June–Sept	purple	medium	loosely bushy, p, bd
Cornflower *Centaurea cyanus*	June–Aug	blue	tall	loosely bushy, a
Cuckooflower *Cardamine pratensis*	April–July	pink	medium	compact, p
Dandelion *Taraxacum officinale*	Mar–Sept	yellow	medium	p
Devil's-bit scabious *Succisa pratensis*	June–Oct	mauve	tall	open and erect, p
Field scabious *Knautia arvensis*	June–Sept	mauve	tall	open, bushy, p
Greater knapweed *Centaurea scabiosa*	July–Sept	purple	tall	open, bushy, p, bd
Heather *Calluna vulgaris*	July–Sept	mauve	tall	bushy shrub, p
Hemp–agrimony *Eupatorium cannabinum*	July–Sept	pink	tall	compact, erect, p
Honeysuckle *Lonicera periclymenum*	June–Sept	cream-pink	tall	rambling shrub, p
Ivy *Hedera helix*	Sept–Nov	green	tall	climber, p
Lucerne *Medicago sativa*	June–July	mauve	tall	open, erect, p
Marjoram *Origanum vulgare*	July–Sept	mauve	tall	open, bushy, p

Pre-eminent as a garden predator is the ladybird. Here, it can be seen eating aphids.

Plant name	Flowering	Colour	Height guide	Type
Musk thistle *Carduus nutans*	May–Aug	purple	tall	open, erect, b
Oxeye daisy *Leucanthemum vulgare*	May–Aug	white	tall	free-flowering, bushy, p, bf
Ragged-robin *Lychnis flos-cuculi*	May–June	red	tall	slender, erect, p
Red campion *Silene dioica*	May–Nov	red	tall	erect, p
Red clover *Trifolium pratense*	May–Sept	red	medium	compact, p
Sainfoin *Onobrychis viciifolia*	May–Aug	pink	medium	open, bushy, p
Saw-wort *Serratula tinctoria*	July–Sept	purple	tall	open, bushy, p
Selfheal *Prunella vulgaris*	June–Sept	purple	medium	p
Small scabious *Scabiosa columbaria*	June–Aug	mauve	medium	open, bushy, p
Soapwort *Saponaria officinalis*	July–Sept	pink	tall	open, erect, p
Thyme *Thymus praecox* subsp. *arcticus*	May–Aug	purple	small	bushy shrub, p
Thrift *Armeria maritima* subsp. *maritima*	April–Aug	pink	small	tufted, p
Teasel *Dipsacus fullonum*	July–Aug	mauve	tall	upright, striking seed heads, b, bd
Vervain *Verbena officinalis*	June–Sept	lilac	medium	loosely bushy, p
White campion *Silene alba*	May–Aug	white	tall	loosely bushy, p, bd
White clover *Trifolium repens*	May–Sept	white	small	compact, creeping, p

Plant name	Flowering	Colour	Height guide	Type
Yarrow *Achillea millefolium*	June–Nov	white	medium	p

Naturalised Flowers

Plant name	Flowering	Colour	Height guide	Type
Dame's-violet *Hesperis matronalis*	May–July	lilac	tall	loosely bushy, b or p
Honesty *Lunaria annua*	April–June	purple	tall	loosely bushy, b
Michaelmas daisy *Aster novi-belgii*	Aug–Oct	blue	tall	compact, erect, p
Red valerian *Centranthus ruber*	May–July	red	tall	loosely bushy, p

White campion

PROTECTED PLANTS

*T*he Wildlife and Countryside Act 1981 gave special protection to a number of native wild plants which were in danger of extinction, either due to their limited numbers, attractiveness to plant collectors or pressure on natural habitats. Some like Cheddar pink are very restricted in their distribution; others are more widespread but both types need the protection of legislation if they are to survive or even, hopefully, increase in number.

Recently, after recommendations made by the Nature Conservancy Council during a regular review provided for under the Act, the list of plants has been increased and now totals 93 species. These are all fully protected, which means that it is a punishable offence to either pick or destroy their flowers or uproot plants. The complete list follows.

There is also a much larger list of threatened species of wild plants given in *British Red Data Book I: Vascular Plants* (Royal Society for Nature Conservation, 2nd edition 1983). These are not legally protected but are in some danger of disappearing unless left alone and undisturbed.

Adder's-tongue spearwort
  Ranunculus ophioglossifolius
Alpine catchfly
  Lychnis alpina
Alpine fleabane
  Erigeron borealis
Alpine gentian
  Gentiana nivalis
Alpine sow-thistle
  Cicicerbita alpina
Alpine rock-cress
  Arabis alpina
Alpine woodsia
  Woodsia alpina
Bedstraw broomrape
  Orobanche caryophyllacea

Blue heath
  Phyllodoce caerulea
Branched horsetail
  Equisetum ramosissimum
Bristol rock-cress
  Arabis stricta
Brown galingale
  Cyperus fuscus
Cambridge milk-parsley
  Selinum carvifolia
Cheddar pink
  Dianthus gratianopolitanus
Childing pink
  Petroraghia nanteuilli
Creeping marshwort
  Apium repens

Cut-leaved germander
Teucrium botrys
Diapensia
Diapensia lapponica
Dickie's bladder-fern
Cystopteris dickieana
Downy woundwort
Stachys germanica
Drooping saxifrage
Saxifraga cernua
Early spider-orchid
Ophrys sphegodes
Early star-of-bethlehem
Gagea bohemica
Fen orchid
Liparis loeselii
Fen ragwort
Senecio paludosus
Fen violet
Viola persicifolia
Field cow-wheat
Melampyrum arvense
Field eryngo
Eryngium campestre
Field wormwood
Artemisia campestris
Fingered speedwell
Veronica triphyllos
Foxtail stonewort
Lamprothamnium papulosum
Fringed gentian
Gentianella ciliata
Ghost orchid
Epipogium aphyllum
Grass-poly
Lythrum hyssopifolia
Greater yellow-rattle
Rhinanthus serotinus
Green hound's-tongue
Cynoglossum germanicum
Holly-leaved naiad
Najas marina
Jersey cudweed
Gnaphalium luteoalbum
Killarney fern
Trichomanes speciosum

Lady's-slipper
Cypripedium calceolus
Late spider-orchid
Ophrys fuciflora
Least adder's-tongue
Ophioglossum lusitanicum
Least lettuce
Lactuca saligna
Limestone woundwort
Stachys alpina
Lizard orchid
Himantoglossum hircinum
Lundy cabbage
Rhynchosinapis wrightii
Martin's ramping-fumitory
Fumaria martinii
Military orchid
Orchis militaris
Monkey orchid
Orchis simia
Norwegian sandwort
Arenaria norvegica
Oblong woodsia
Woodsia ilvensis
Oxtongue broomrape
Orobanche loricata
Pennyroyal
Mentha pulegium
Perennial knawel
Scleranthus perennis
Pigmyweed
Crassula aquatica
Plymouth pear
Pyrus cordata
Purple colt's-foot
Homogyne alpina
Purple spurge
Euphorbia peplis
Red-tipped cudweed
Filago lutescens
Red helleborine
Cephalanthera rubra
Ribbon-leaved water-plantain
Alisma gramineum
Rock cinquefoil
Potentilla rupestris

Rough marsh-mallow
Althaea hirsuta
Round-headed leek
Allium sphaerocephalon
Sand crocus
Romulea columnae
Sea knotgrass
Polygonum maritimum
Sea-lavender
Limonium paradoxum
Sea-lavender
Limonium recurvum
Sickle-leaved hare's-ear
Bupleurum falcatum
Slender cottongrass
Eriophorum gracile
Small alison
Alyssum alyssoides
Small fleabane
Pulicaria vulgaris
Small hare's-ear
Bupleurum baldense
Small restharrow
Ononis reclinata
Snowdon lily
Lloydia serotina
Spiked speedwell
Veronica spicata
Spring gentian
Gentiana verna
Starfruit
Damasonium alisma
Starved wood-sedge
Carex depauperata
Stinking goosefoot
Chenopodium vulvaria
Stinking hawk's-beard
Crepis foetida
Strapwort
Corrigiola litoralis
Teesdale sandwort
Minuartia stricta
Thistle broomrape
Orobanche reticulata
Triangular club-rush
Scirpus triquetrus

Tufted saxifrage
Saxifraga cespitosa
Viper's-grass
Scorzonera humilis
Water germander
Teucrium scordium
Whorled Solomon's-seal
Polygonatum verticillatum
Wild cotoneaster
Cotoneaster integerrimus
Wild gladiolus
Gladiolus illyricus
Wood calamint
Calamintha sylvatica
Young's helleborine
Epipactis youngiana

Large-flowered evening-primrose

USEFUL ADDRESSES

*L*isted below are organisations concerned with the preservation and/or cultivation of wild flowers and the protection of wildlife.

The British Butterfly Conservation Society
Tudor House,
Quorn,
Loughborough,
Leics LE12 8AD
Tel. 0509 412870

Council for the Protection of Rural England (CPRE)
4 Hobart Place,
London SW1

Farming and Wildlife Group
The Lodge,
Sandy,
Beds SG19 2DL
Tel. 0767 80551

Fauna and Flora Preservation Society
c/o Zoological Gardens,
Regent's Park,
London NW1 4RY
Tel. 01 387 9656

Hardy Plant Society
10 St Barnabas Road,
Emmer Green,
Reading,
Berks

Henry Doubleday Research Association
Ryton-on-Dunsmore,
Coventry CV8 3LG
Tel. 0203 303517

Herb Society
77 great Peter Street,
London SW1P 2EZ

Land Life
Old Police Station,
Lark Lane,
Liverpool 17
Tel. 051728 7011

National Council for the Conservation of Plants and Gardens
c/o RHS,
Wisley,
Woking,
Surrey GU23 6QB

Nature Conservancy Council
Northminster House,
Peterborough PE1 1UA
Tel. 0733 40345

Royal Horticultural Society
Vincent Square,
London SW1P 2PE
Tel. 01 834 4333

Royal Society for Nature Conservation
The Green,
Nettleham,
Lincoln LN2 2NR
Tel. 0522 752326

Royal Society for the Protection of Birds
The Lodge,
Sandy,
Beds SG19 2DL
Tel. 0767 80551

Urban Wildlife Group
11 Albert Street,
Birmingham B4 7UA
Tel. 021 236 3626

Wild Flower Society
68 Outwoods Road,
Loughborough,
Leics LE11 3LY

Woodland Trust
Autumn Park,
Dysart Road,
Grantham,
Lincs NG31 6LL
Tel. 0476 74297

World Wildlife Fund
Panda House,
Wayside Park,
Godalming,
Surrey GU7 1XR
Tel. 04834 26444

Young People's Trust for Endangered Species
19 Quarry Street,
Guildford,
Surrey GU1 3EH
Tel. 0483 39600

International Bee Research Association
18 North Road,
Cardiff CF1 3DY

◆ SUPPLIERS ◆

◆ Key to abbreviations

Sp = specialist wild flower seed suppliers
S = separately packeted species
M = packeted flower seed mixtures
G = packeted flower and grass seed mixtures
B = bulk flower species and flower and grass seed for sowing large areas
P = mail order catalogue for packets available (send sae)
T = trade lists for bulk available

◆ Wild flower seed packet specialists

Ashton Wold Seeds Project
Ashton Wold,
Ashton,
Peterborough PE8 5LE
Tel. 0832 73575
B T (trade suppliers only)

Booker Seeds Ltd
Boston Road,
Sleaford,
Lincs
B T (trade suppliers only)

British Seed Houses Ltd
Bewsey Industrial Estate,
Pitt Street,
Warrington,
Cheshire WA5 5LE
Tel. 0925 54411
B T (trade suppliers only)

Carters Ltd
Hele Road,
Torquay,
Devon TQ2 7QJ
Tel. 0803 62011
S M (shop and garden centre suppliers
only)

John Chambers' Wild Flower Seeds
15 Westleigh Road,
Barton Seagrave,
Kettering,
Northants NN15 5AJ
Tel. 0933 681632
Sp S M G B P T (mail order, shop and
garden centre and trade suppliers)

Chiltern Seeds
Bortree Stile,
Ulverston,
Cumbria LA12 7PB
S P (mail order suppliers only)

Cuthberts Ltd
Hele Road,
Torquay,
Devon TQ2 7QJ
Tel. 0803 62011
    S (shop and garden centre suppliers
    only)

Samuel Dobie & Son Ltd
PO Box 90,
Paignton,
Devon TQ3 1XY
Tel. 0803 616281
S M P (mail order suppliers only)

Emorsgate Seeds
Terrington Court,
Terrington St Clement,
Kings Lynn,
Norfolk PE34 4NT
Tel. 0553 829028
Sp B T (trade suppliers only)

Fisons PLC Horticulture Division
Paper Mill Lane,
Bramford,
Ipswich,
Suffolk IP8 4BS
Tel. 0473 830492
S M (shop and garden centre suppliers
only)

Mr Fothergill's Seeds Ltd
Kentford,
Newmarket,
Suffolk CB8 7BR
Tel. 0638 751161
S M G P (mail order and shop and garden
centre suppliers only)

Heritage Seeds,
Lodge Cottage,
Osmington,
Weymouth,
Dorset DT3 6EX
B

Hurst
Unit 7,
Cromwell Centre,
Stepfield,
Witham,
Essex CM8 3TA
Tel. 0376 515811
S M (shop and garden centre suppliers
only)

W. W. Johnson Ltd
London Road,
Boston,
Lincs PE21 8AD
Tel. 0205 65051
Sp S M G B T (shop and garden centre
   and trade suppliers only)

Naturescape
Little Orchard,
Main Street,
Whatton in the Vale,
Notts NG13 9EP
Tel. 0949 51045
Sp S M G B P T (mail order and trade
   suppliers only)

Mommersteeg International
Station Road,
Finedon,
Wellingborough,.
Northants NN9 5NT
Tel. 0933 680891
B T (trade suppliers only)

Suffolk Herbs
Sawyers Farm, Little Cornard,
Sudbury,
Suffolk CO10 0NY
Tel. 0787 227247
Sp S M G B P T (mail order, shop and
   garden centre and trade suppliers only)

Sutton's Seeds Ltd
Hele Road,
Torquay,
Devon TQ2 7QJ
Tel. 0803 62011
S M P (mail order and shop and garden
   centre suppliers only)

Thompson & Morgan
London Road,
Ipswich,
Suffolk IP2 0BA
Tel. 0473 688588
S M P (mail order and shop and garden
   suppliers only)

Unwins Seeds Ltd
Histon,
Cambridge CB4 4LE
Tel. 022023 2270
S P (shop and garden centre suppliers
   only)

◆ **Suppliers of wild flower plants**

Ashton Wold Seeds Project
(*see above*)
T

Barn Plants
Fornham Road Farm,
Great Barton,
Bury St Edmunds,
Suffolk IP31 2SD
Tel. 028487 317
P T

John Chambers
(*see above*, also wild flower bulbs)
P T

Emorsgate Seeds
(*see above*)
T

Mr Fothergill's Seeds
(*see above*)
P

Landlife Wild Flowers Ltd
The Old Police Station,
Lark Lane,
Liverpool L17 8UU
Tel. 051 728 7011
T

Naturescape
(*see above*)
P

NPK Landscape Architects
542 Parrs Wood Road,
East Didsbury,
Manchester M20 0QA
Tel: 061 794 9314
T

Paradise Centre
Twinstead Road,
Lamarsh,
Bures,
Suffolk CO8 5EX
Tel. 078729 449

G & J E Peacock
Kingsfield Tree Nursery,
Broadenham Lane,
Winsham,
Chard,
Somerset TA20 4JF
Tel. 046030 697
T

Stapeley Water Gardens Ltd
London Road,
Stapeley,
Nantwich,
Cheshire CW5 7JL
Tel. 0270 623868
P T (specialise in native wetland and water
    plants)

Ruth Thompson
Oak Cottage Herb Farm,
Nesscliffe,
Shropshire DY4 1DB
Tel. 074381 262
P

◆ **Wild flower gardens**

Craft at the Suffolk Barn
Fornham Road,
Bury St Edmunds,
Suffolk IP31 2SD
Tel. 028487 317
(semi-formal demonstration herb and wild
    flower garden attached to East Anglian
    craft centre and tea shop)

Careby Manor Gardens
Careby,
Stamford,
Lincs PE9 4EA
Tel. 078081 2200
(Cottage garden with wild flowers and old-
    fashioned roses)

Selfheal

INDEX

Figures in *italics* refer to colour illustrations, figures in **bold** refer to the plant's main entry.

WHAT IS THE WI?

If you have enjoyed this book, the chances are that you would enjoy belonging to the largest women's organisation in the country – the Women's Institutes.

We are friendly, go-ahead, like-minded women, who derive enormous satisfaction from all the movement has to offer. This list is long – you can make new friends, have fun and companionship, visit new places, develop new skills, take part in community services, fight local campaigns, become a WI market producer, and play an active role in an organisation which has a national voice.

The WI is the only women's organisation in the country which owns an adult education establishment. At Denman College, you can take a course in anything from car maintenance to paper sculpture, from book-binding to yoga, or word processing to the martial arts.

All you need to do to join is write to us here at the **National Federation of Women's Institutes, 39 Eccleston Street, London SW1W 9NT,** or telephone 01-730 7212, and we will put you in touch with WIs in your immediate locality.

About the author

John Chambers is the leading specialist supplier of wild flower seeds to the public and, for the last ten years, has operated his own mail order and wholesale business. He attends many agricultural and horticultural shows and won a gold medal at Chelsea Flower Show for his Gale's Honey Bee Garden; he also won a gold at the 1986 Stoke Garden Festival. John Chambers lectures widely to a number of organisations including garden clubs, universities, conservation groups and Women's Institutes.